POCKET THEOLOGY

by

Voltaire

Translated from the French
by Miss Ellen Carroll

THE BOOK TREE
San Diego, California

Previous edition published 1912
The Truth Seeker Company
New York

New updated edition
Contains modern spellings, updated language & new format
New material, revisions and cover
© 2015 The Book Tree
All rights reserved

No part of this publication may be used or transmitted in any way without the expressed written consent of the publisher, except for short excerpts for use in reviews.

ISBN 978-1-58509-360-1

Main cover image copyright by kai4107
distorted cross image © Sutham

Cover layout by
Mike Sparrow

Published by
The Book Tree
P O Box 16476
San Diego, CA 92176
www.thebooktree.com

We provide fascinating and educational products to help awaken the public to new ideas and information that would not be available otherwise.

Call 1 (800) 700-8733 for our FREE BOOK TREE CATALOG.

Introduction

This is a collection of religious quotes, aphorisms and definitions that are arranged alphabetically. It serves as a pocket dictionary of theology like none other found today. Virtually everything Voltaire wrote during his life that concerned religion was immediately banned, so this collection of highlights will allow the reader to understand why his views met with such hostility. Despite his critical slant, most of the entries make surprising sense. Even devout Christians will chuckle knowingly from time to time while reading through this book. No person or religion is perfect and Voltaire was able to use his sharp wit and sarcasm to point out these imperfections. Instead of making us primarily angry at religious authority, he gives us the ability to laugh at their follies or ignorance. Some sections may still incite a bit of anger, however. Otherwise, how could it be Voltaire?

The more one knows of Christianity, the more interesting this collection becomes. For example, under "PETER," it is explained that Jesus made a pun of Peter's name, which ultimately gave the Pope his kitchen (or place in Rome). Voltaire failed to explain the details behind this pun, which had otherwise helped cause the belief that Peter was the first Pope. There is no evidence to show that Peter was ever in Rome, much less having been the first Pope. Voltaire was clearly aware that Jesus' quote, "upon this rock I will build my church," was a pun of sorts. It was not meant to mean Peter in the literal sense, which most scholars have agreed upon. (For a complete explanation and verification, see my contributed chapter to *The Book No Pope Would Want You to Read*, editors Tim Leedom & Maryjane Churchville, eworld, Inc., 2010.)

It is not recommended to give this book to friends as a companion to their Bibles — unless they have a sense of humor. It should not be given out at church, but should instead be kept in a place where one can laugh freely without having to explain oneself to serious believers. Your idea of fun, or what is funny, may not be the same as your local minister's or your aunt Martha's. With this in mind, please proceed to enjoy one of the greatest and sharpest minds to have ever graced this earth — a legend if you will… Voltaire.

Paul Tice

POCKET THEOLOGY

AARON

The high priest of the Hebrews, the worthy brother of Moses, and the perfect pattern of our modern priests. He caused his followers to worship, and he himself worshiped, the golden calf, an example that has been pretty closely imitated by the majority of his sacerdotal successors, even down to the present day. For his want of faith he was forbidden to see the Promised Land, which, probably, accounts for the slight faith of his successors in the promises of future bliss they so liberally hold out to believers. However, in spite of these drawbacks, God knew so well the value of a high priest that he showed himself deeply interested even with regard to the number of bells that he was to wear on his petticoats. This should teach us that nothing concerning his ministers is indifferent to God.

ABBEYS

Sacred retreats from the corruptions of the world, built and endowed at divers periods of quickened faith by pious brigands, and destined to receive a certain number of very useful citizens and citizenesses, who consecrated themselves to singing, eating, and sleeping, all to the end that their fellow-citizens should succeed in their labors.

ABBOT

A spiritual father, in the enjoyment of a temporal income — attached to an abbey — on condition that he shall read his breviary, torment the monks, and go to law with them. Every abbot in this world is not in the enjoyment of an abbey, though he would very much like to be so. A goodly number are only in the enjoyment of the right of going about dressed in black, wearing a linen band round their necks, and retailing items of the news of what is going on in the world.

ABNEGATION

A Christian virtue; the effect of divine grace. It consists in hating one's self; detesting every species of pleasure; avoiding everything that is pleasant and agreeable as if it were the plague itself, all of which becomes quite easy if the subject has received a dose of grace sufficient to deprive him of his wits.

ABRAHAM

The father of all the faithful. He lied, and was made a cuckold; he pared off his foreskin, and, in a word, gave proof of so much faith that, had it not been for angelic intervention in the nick of time, he would have cut the throat of his own son, whom the Lord, in a jesting mood, had commanded him to sacrifice. God then made a covenant with him and with his seed forever; but the Son of God afterwards annulled this treaty for some good reasons that his papa did not foresee when he made it.

ABSOLUTION

The remission of the sins we have committed against God. The priests of the Romish Church grant it to sinners in virtue of a blank check from the divinity itself; a most happy invention, well calculated to reassure certain timorous rogues who might be inclined to feel remorse for their shortcomings did not the Mother Church thus take the trouble to set them entirely at their ease on that score.

ABSTINENCE

A most pious practice which consists in depriving ourselves of the benefits of divine Providence, who created all good things to the sole end of preventing his creatures from enjoying them. Thus it is that by commanding us to abstain the Church merely remedies the too lavish goodness of God.

ABSURDITIES

There can be none such in religion, which is the work of the Word, or the Divine Reason, which, as we all know, has nothing in common with human reason. It is only through want of faith that incredulous persons fancy they can perceive absurdities in Christianity, whence it results that a want of faith is the height of absurdity. The absurdities of the Christian belief disappear when its doctrines have been inculcated from earliest childhood and adhered to without doubt or question. The more absurd a thing may appear to the eyes of human reason, the more fit and proper does it appear to the eyes of divine reason, or, in other words, of religion.

ABUSES

Abuses will here and there creep into the Church in spite of the divine vigilance. The only thing to be done in such cases is to reform such abuse or abuses when they have become too notorious to be any longer upheld. For the rest, it is only the incredulous who can detect such abuses, the eyes of believers being blind to them.

ADAM

He was the first man. God created him a big booby, who, to please his wife, was stupid enough to devour an apple which his descendants have never since been able to digest.

ADVENT

A time of fasting, mortification, and tears, during which all good Christians grieve and mourn over the near coming of their Savior.

AGNUS DEL

Small cakes of wax much revered by Roman Catholics, and blessed by the pope himself, consequently having received from the fountain-head the miraculous power of driving out devils, exorcising witchcraft, and stilling storms and tempests. This is why thunderbolts have never been known to fall in localities in possession of this blessed commodity.

ALIENATION

The property of the Church cannot be alienated, the priests being but the guardians thereof, and God himself the proprietor. His ministers, therefore, have the power to alienate nothing, save and except their own wits and the wits of those who listen to their pious teachings.

ALMS

A distribution of one's own possessions, or of somebody else's to the end of perpetuating the pious leisure of priests, monks, and other lazy folk who find it much more agreeable and convenient to pray than to work.

ALTARS

God's tables, upon which he, disgusted with the meats formerly served up to him, now requires that his sacrificers shall serve up to him his own Son, of whom they (the sacrificers) likewise partake and cause others to partake. The sight of this delicate repast disarms the Eternal Father of his anger and inspires him with the friendliest sentiments for all who thus sit at his table and gobble up portions of his beloved Son under his very nose.
The altar, in a figurative sense, is always opposed to the throne, which means that priests are often more cunning than potentates. In the meantime it is the custom, whenever the Church is attacked, to proclaim with a loud voice that both the altar and the throne are in danger. In this manner the Church is rendered interesting, and potentates are led to consider themselves as bound in honor to espouse her quarrels and to interest themselves in her affairs, even to the detriment of their own interests.

ANATHEMA

A species of charitable curse launched by the ministers of a God of peace against all or any that displease them — devoting those to eternal torments for the good of their souls when they cannot get a chance of torturing their bodies.

ANCHORITES

Very holy men, and justly held in esteem and veneration by the Church, who withdrew themselves from all commerce with the world, in the fear of incurring the misfortune of being of any good to it.

ANGELS

The messengers of the celestial cabinet whom God dispatches to his favorites here below. Without the angels, God would be obliged to do his own errands. Every Christian enjoys the privilege of having a guardian angel all to himself, who would prevent him from doing many foolish things were it not for the principle of man's free will, which cannot be set aside. Archangels are to angels what archbishops are to bishops: the Divinity employs them on its most important missions.

ANGER

A deadly sin in a layman, who should only get angry when the Church gets angry, because then it is God himself who gets angry. In truth, the God of all goodness is an angry God, whose beloved children are created in wrath. It is therefore mete and proper that the latter should get angry when he is so himself, otherwise he might get angry if his creatures were less angry than he. Priests are the surest thermometers of the divine wrath.

ANNATS (first fruits)

Catholic sovereigns wisely allow a foreign priest to fleece the priests of their own states. Otherwise the latter could not, in their turn, exercise the divine right of fleecing their fellow-citizens.

ANNUNCIATION

A visit of ceremony paid by a pure spirit to a virgin of Judea, accompanied with a pretty compliment. The result was a fine brat, as big as his papa, who has since made a certain noise in the world, and, there is room to hope, will make a great deal more if mankind continues to be as good and wise as it has been hitherto.

ANTHROPOLOGY

A way of explaining themselves peculiar to our sacred writers, and which consists in endowing with eyes, hands, passions, and wicked malice the pure spirit that rules the universe. God created man in his own image, and the priests have made God in the image of the priests. This is, possibly, why we love them so.

ANTILOGY

A theological term to designate the contradictions to be found from time to time in the Word of God. These contradictions are but apparent, of course, and none but stone-blind people can detect them. People of enlightened faith can perceive at once that God cannot contradict himself, unless, indeed, his ministers cause him to change his mind.

ANTIPODES

To believe in the antipodes constitutes a wicked heresy. God, who made the world, ought to have known if there were such a thing, and it is evident from his books that he did not believe in it.

ANTIQUITY

Is infallible, and cannot err. Its antiquity is the indubitable proof of the soundness of an opinion, of a custom, or a ceremony. It is highly important to repulse and discourage all attempts at innovation. Old shoes are more commodious and easy to the feet than new ones. The clergy must never relinquish whatever they have hitherto practiced. The more ancient the church, the more prone is she to wander both in action and discourse.

APOCALYPSE

A very curious and worthy book of Holy Writ, commented by Newton, and containing a series of tales invented by St. John, of a rather less cheerful character than the fables of LaFontaine, but infinitely better calculated to stir the minds of the grown-up children who read them. During three centuries the Greek Church persisted in regarding the Apocalypse as an apocryphal book, but the Latin Fathers, much more knowing, have declared it sacred, thereby confirming its right of canonization.

APOSTLES

A dozen of knaves, as ignorant as owls and as poor as church mice, who composed the court of the Son of God here below, and were charged by him to teach the universe. Their successors have since risen in the world, thanks to theology, which their predecessors, the apostles, had not studied. For the rest, the clergy, like the aristocracy, is so constituted as to derive a greater degree of luster in proportion as they recede from their primitive origin, or the resemblance between them and their predecessors fades away.

APPARITIONS

Supernatural visions permitted to him or her gifted by God with the special grace of possessing a cracked brain, a hysterical temperament, a disordered digestion, but, above all, the art of lying with effrontery.

APPEAL

An impious custom, and offensive to the Church, wickedly established in certain countries, where the people have the temerity to appeal to profane judges against the decisions of saintly ones, who are, as it is well known, incapable of abusing their authority or ministry.

APPELLANTS

These are, in France, the Jansenists who have advisedly appealed against the bull *Unigenitus* to the future Council General which shall settle definitively all disputes touching divine grace. According to the latest news, this council will be held without fail on the eve of the Day of Judgment.

ARCHBISHOP

A title unknown in the earlier centuries of the Church, but invented since by the humility of her pastors, who, after having raised themselves up on the backs of the profane, endeavored to climb on each other's backs to see what was passing in the fold of the Lord.

ARK OF GOD

The cash-box of the clergy. There is no joking with God touching this same cash-box of his spouse, which contains all the property and jewels of the community. Were it not for the faith that sustains them, princes, who are sometimes "hard up," might be tempted to lay hands on it. However, by going the right way about it, they might try the thing. God, who sometimes slumbers, might perhaps let them carry off the strong box without giving the alarm.

ARMS

The clergy may not carry arms themselves, but, in case of need, may place them in the hands of laymen to do battle in the cause of Mother Church, who, at a safe distance, raises her pious hands to heaven to implore its aid in favor of those who are fighting for her divine rights or the gratification of her sacred whims.

ARM (Secular)

A monarch, a magistrate, a policeman, or a hangman, to whom the Church, tender mother, may hand over any one of the children that offend her and whom she has not the heart to murder herself.

ASSASSINATION

A case involving the criminal dock with regard to the laity, but privileged with regard to the clergy. In some countries the latter enjoy the right of thieving and assassination in utter defiance of ordinary justice. Moreover, the Church enjoys by divine right the right of assassinating heretics, tyrants, and miscreants, or at least of causing them to be assassinated by the laity, she herself abhorring bloodshed.

ASSES

Long-eared animals, patient and humble, and the true models to be imitated by all good Christians, who, like them, must allow themselves to be saddled with their burdens and carry their cross. Jesus was mounted on an ass which did not belong to him when he entered into Jerusalem, by which action he intended to proclaim to all whom it might concern that the priests should thenceforward enjoy the right of riding on the backs of Christians to the end of all time.

ATHEIST

A name given by theologians to whoever differs from them in their ideas concerning the divinity, or who refuses to believe in it in the form in which, in the emptiness of their infallible pates, they have resolved to present it to him. As a rule, an Atheist is any or every man who does not believe in the God of the priests.

ATTRIBUTES (Divine)

Incomprehensible qualities which, by dint of reflecting on, our theologians have decided can only belong to a being of whom they have not the least idea. These qualities seem incompatible to persons of weak faith, but are easily reconcilable to those who do not reflect about them. The negative attributes with which theology has endowed the Godhead clearly demonstrate that the divinity can have no possible resemblance to any being or thing we can possibly imagine. This is conclusive, and eminently calculated to settle our ideas on this point.

AUGURS

How our modern augurs must enjoy themselves when, glass in hand, they devise among them of the folly of all who are not, as they are, members of the college of augurs!

AUSTERITY

An ingenious means invented by perfected Christians of rendering themselves agreeable in the sight of a God of infinite goodness by torturing themselves with fastings, flagellations, etc. God is, of course, always delighted with such like inventions in his honor on the part of his creatures. Austerities are, moreover, advantageous and profitable, inasmuch as they create an extreme wonder in those who are witnesses of these marvelous follies, while, on the other hand, the meek and pure of faith regard them as both wise and good.

AUTHORITY (Ecclesiastical)

A faculty enjoyed by God's ministers to convince us of the wisdom of their decisions, of the authenticity of their rights, and the soundness of their opinions by the help of prisons, soldiers, stakes, fagots, and *lettres-de-cachet*.

AUTO-DA-FE

An act of faith. A dainty feast offered to the Divinity from time to time, and which consisted of roasting, in great pomp, the bodies of Jews or heretics for the salvation of their souls and the edification of the lookers-on. From this we may infer that the Father of Mercies has ever shown a marked taste for roasts and broils.

AVARICE

A deadly sin in the laity, who should invariably show themselves generous and open-handed towards Mother Church; as for the latter, she may not emulate them in this wise, inasmuch as her possessions all belong to her spouse, who might grumble and storm were she to show too much indulgence or generosity to such arrant rogues as they.

AVE MARIA

An elegant and well-turned compliment paid by the angel Gabriel to the Virgin Mary, on the part of God the Father, on announcing to her that she was about to conceive of the Holy Ghost. Since her death, or her assumption, this virgin, it would seem, is always extremely gratified whenever any mention is made of this episode in her life, and which, for the rest, does her a great deal of credit.

AZYMOUS (unleavened) BREAD

Once upon a time there arose in the Church an important dissension touching the preference given by God to leavened or unleavened bread as the agent of his transformation in the ceremony of the Mass. This great question, after having for a vast length of time divided the universe, is now happily settled, one portion of the Christians using leavened bread for the purpose, and the others azymous, or unleavened, bread.

BABEL (Tower of)

A parable of allegory, under which, to judge from all appearances, the Bible prophetically designated theology, thereby giving to understand that all who raise themselves up to the Godhead and discuss among themselves of his essence and attributes will no more understand each other than a Hottentot would a Frenchman, a curate his bishop, or a Molinist a Jansenist.

BALAAM

A false prophet whose ass, it is said, possessed the gift of speech. Strong-minded people, of course, will not believe this, notwithstanding the fact that this miracle has been perpetuated in the Church, where nothing is more ordinary than to see asses, both male and female, speak and even reason on questions of theology.

BAPTISM

A sacrament absolutely indispensable to salvation. God will receive none into his glory unless once in their lives they have received a douche of cold water on the occiput. This water has the virtue of cleansing an infant of an enormous sin expiated by the Son of God and which had been committed but a few thousand years before the parents of the child dreamed of making him.

BASTARDS

Scapegraces whose parents have not paid the Church to purchase the right of lying together. In accordance with the wise jurisdiction introduced by original sin, all such are denied the advantages enjoyed by those whose parents *have* paid to lie together.

BEADLE

A man in the service of the Church, and, like the priest, deriving a living from the altar. It is popularly believed that the beadle makes his soup with the consecrated bread.

BEATIFICATION

A solemn act by which the Roman pontiff, who receives the most authentic news from the other world, declares to the universe that some monk he never before heard of, enjoys eternal felicity, and has to be complimented accordingly.

BELIEF

An unlimited confidence and faith in priests. A good Christian should believe all that he is told to believe, otherwise he is only good for the stake. If he objects that he has not been gifted with the grace to believe, burn him all the same, for by denying him such grace the Divinity clearly demonstrates that he considers him as only fit to be made a bonfire of to warm the faith in the hearts of his elect.

BELLS

Noisy theological instruments, destined, like the priests, to deafen and bewilder the living, while calling upon the dead to "pay up" their debts to the Church. Bells are very good Christians, seeing that they are always baptized. We may even go so far as to assume that they keep their baptismal innocence pure and unspotted, which the generality of other Christians do not.

BENCHES

Wooden seats upon which theologians rest their pious posteriors, and often throw at each other's heads in their friendly discussions on religion.

BENEDICTIONS

Charms, sorceries, and magical ceremonies, by the aid of which the ministers of the most high, while holding up two fingers in space and mumbling divers holy conjurations, evoke the Almighty and prevail on him to turn on the tap of his grace on men and things here below, which above all fills even to overflowing the pockets of the clergy. Once a thing has been blessed it is sacred, it ceases to be profane, and thenceforward cannot be touched without sacrilege and profanation — crimes that deserve the stake.

BENEFICES

Revenues attached to an ecclesiastical office and collected in the name of God by a member of the clergy, who, as soon as he has got them, possesses them by right divine, and consequently is under no obligation to anybody. A priest cannot possess more than one benefice, a rule of the Church which is, as we all know, one of the most strictly observed.

BIBLE

A most sacred book, of divine inspiration, and containing all that a Christian should know and practice. It is not seemly that laymen should read it, as the word of God could not fail to do them harm. It is much wiser that the priests read it for them, they alone having stomachs vigorous enough to digest it. Laymen should be content with the products of the sacerdotal digestion.

BLASPHEMIES

Words or discourses which attach to unknown objects ideas that are not fitting to them, or which deprive them of the idea that the priests have judged fitting to them. Whence it results that to blaspheme is to differ in opinion to the clergy, clearly one of the most horrible of crimes.

BRAINS

A good Christian should have no brains, or at least the less he has of them the better. With the help of preceptors, confessors, and convents, Christian parents can have the brains of their offspring reduced to the least volume.

BREVIARY

A selection of prayers, in elegant Latin, that the priests, the bestowers of blessings, to gain their salary, are obliged to recite every day, under pain of being useless to society.

BROTHER

All men are brothers, that is to say, constantly quarreling among themselves about the inheritance left them by their father whose will, of meaning passably obscure in the origin, has been rendered a great deal more so by the theologians.

BISHOP

A word that signifies inspector. A priest who, like certain insects, possesses the faculty of reproducing and multiplying his species without the aid of a female. The episcopate is so heavy a burden that it is only with the greatest repugnance that a reverend will consent to undertake a charge which he has been begging for for years, notwithstanding.

BLOOD

The Church abhors the sight of blood. She would faint at the sight of a single drop, but has no objection to its being shed in torrents by the magistrate and the hangman, who are her surgeons-in-chief.

BOOK OF LIFE

A little register of great brevity in which the Most High, to help his memory, writes down, or causes to be written by his chief secretary, the names of all those of his creatures who, in each succeeding century here below, were lucky enough to satisfy him and do homage and honor to his priests.

BOOKS

The Church needs no other books than those used in the choirs. Idiots may also be permitted to read the *Imitation of Jesus Christ* and their prayer books. All other species of literature should be burnt or placed in the libraries of convents and monasteries, where they can harm no one.

BULLS

Strips of parchment invested with a leaden seal which the servant of the servants of God dispatches whenever there is question either of raising money or of exciting a religious fermentation in localities that may happen to be in need of exercise. Had it not been for the bull *Unigenitus*, France would have been plunged in the most frightful torpor.

BURDEN

The burden of the Lord is light. The priests make us carry this burden for them, which prevents them from feeling the weight thereof, or rather, it is the priests themselves who, according to Jeremy, are in reality the burden of the Lord.

CALAMITIES

Sinister events permitted by the Divine Will to afflict humanity to the greater honor and profit of the priests. Nations, like individuals, are never so devout as when they are frightened or very miserable. In order that the clergy should have a real subject of satisfaction, calamities, especially those in the form of contagion, should happen a little more frequently than they do, for then they might fall into real good things, or at least have the pleasure of burying everybody.

CALENDS (Greek)

A certain period to which the faithful are referred by the priests for the verification of the efficacy of their breviary, the authenticity of their rights, and the utility of their lessons.

CALUMNY

A most legitimate weapon piously employed by priests and other devotees, male and female, but especially female, against the enemies of their confessors and of the Church, and all to the greater honor and glory of the God of all truth.

CANONICAL (books)

All the books contained in the Bible and recognized by the Church, and which the priests have, with their own eyes, seen the Holy Spirit himself write down.

CANONIZATION

A solemn ceremony by which the holy Father, induced by the miracles worked by some holy men, dead and buried a hundred years ago, or by the money of those interested in his reputation, notifies all whom it may concern that this same man is in Paradise, that the faithful may, in all security, burn candles in his honor, and give the wherewithal to the monks to "liquor up" to the same effect.

CANONS

Rules and decisions by which the bishops, assembled in council, fix for the time being the immutable dogmas of the faith, the discipline of the Church, explain, revise, and correct the word of God, create titles and incontestable rights for themselves, curse all who dare to call such in question, and meet with the promptest obedience when the cannons of princes come to the aid of the canons of the Church.

CAPUCHIN (friar)

A two-legged he-goat, laden with ignorance, filth, and vermin, who sings through his nose inside of his monastery and shows himself abroad to the edification of old women and the terror of little children.

CARDINAL

A priest who is scarlet from head to foot, and who, by virtue of a pope's brief, becomes the equal of kings and withdraws himself from the jurisdiction of the latter, except in cases where there are questions of receiving favors from their hands, which favors he only accepts from pure civility. Cardinals are clothed in red, or flame color, to keep forever before their eyes the blood that must be shed for the good of the Church and the fagots that must be lighted for the maintenance of the faith.

CARMELITES

An order of monks who, by special grace, are gifted with unknown talents which they would make known if the faith had not declined on the earth.

CARNAL

That which is not spiritual. Carnal men are those who have not mind enough to appreciate spiritual benefits, for which they are told to renounce earthly happiness. As a rule, carnal men are all who have the misfortune to be made of flesh and blood, and are gifted with common sense.

CASUISTS

Spiritual mathematicians who have contrived to calculate and reduce to equations the sins that a good Christian may commit without making the Divinity too mad with him.

CATECHISM

A collection of pious, intelligible, and necessary instructions that priests take care to inculcate into little Christians to the end that they may talk nonsense and rave for the rest of their lives.

CATHOLIC

Signifies universal. The Catholic, or universal Church is the church of which at least three-quarters and a half of the human race have never yet heard mention and whose ministers, by a special gift of grace, seldom or never agree among themselves, a clear proof that the truths they proclaim were not concerted by them and agreed upon beforehand.

CAUSE (of God)

Is the cause of the priests, who, as we all know, are his advocates and stewards; but who, it would seem, have but very seldom received from him full powers to transact his business with mildness or gentleness.

CAUSES (final)

Theologians are the confidants of the Most High; they know the motives of all his actions, and assure us that if there are plagues, wars, famines, mosquitoes, bed-bugs, and theological bickerings here below it is even for the greater good and well-being of mankind. Anyway, it is quite sure that whatever happens in this world invariably turns to the greater advantage and profit of the priests — God, in all his works, having in view the benefit of none other than of his clergy.

CELIBACY

A correction wisely made by the Romish Church to the command given by God himself to the human race to increase and multiply. Thus, a sincere Christian ought not to marry. As for the priests, they need no wives, the laity having a number sufficient for both. A married priest would run the risk of having interests in common with his fellow-citizens, a state of things not at all in keeping with the profound and sacred views of the Holy Catholic Church, apostolic and Roman.

CEMETERIES

Consecrated grounds blessed by the Church, and in which, till the resurrection of the dead, she permits her dead children to rot in the open air when they have not money enough to buy the right to rot in a mausoleum and to infect the living. As the rich but seldom go to heaven, it is only civil to lodge them, if they pay, while awaiting the Day of Judgment.

CENOBITES

Monks who live in company that they may the more effectually enrage and make each other mad, thereby attaining to the kingdom of heaven, which is only to be attained by those who are very mad indeed, here below.

CENSER

A sacred pan in which perfumes are burned to regale the nostrils of the Most High. The priests are the privileged perfumers. "To put one's hand in the censer" is a pure metaphor which designates the detestable crime of which a prince or magistrate would be guilty by impertinently poking his nose into priestly affairs before being invited to do so.

CENSURE

A stigmatizing gratification bestowed by theologians on persons or books that may happen to disagree with them, the theologians, or their infallible ideas. We do not suppose for a moment that this little dictionary will fall under such censure.

CEREMONIES

Movements of the body wisely ordained by the priests to the end of being agreeable to God. These ceremonies are of so much importance that it would be better for a nation to perish by fire and sword than to omit or change a single one.

CERTITUDE

The evidence of the fact that the anointed of the Lord can neither delude themselves nor others; hence it is that theological certitude is much better founded than physical certitude, which has no other vouchers than our senses, which are liable to deceive us.

CHAIR (holy)

A species of night-stool upon which a newly-elected pope places his reverend posterior to the end of having his sex verified and thus avoiding the embarrassments that might accrue to the Church should she unwittingly elect a popess.

CHANT

The Most High has a decided taste for vocal music, provided it be lugubrious and gloomy enough. Hence it is that Christians spend so much of their wealth to have bawled into his ears night and day psalmodies which sound to profane ears as of a most harassing and aggravating character.

CHARITY

Is the greatest of all the Christian virtues, and consists in loving with our whole hearts a God with whom we have but the very slightest acquaintance, or his priests, with whom we are very well

Pocket Theology 29

acquainted indeed. It moreover requires us to love our neighbor as ourselves, that is, provided he loves God and his priests and is beloved by them, otherwise it is charity to murder him. But the most genuine and efficacious charity is that which greases the paws of the priests; such charity covereth a multitude of sins.

CHASTITY

A virtue most piously observed by the priests, monks, and monkesses in Italy, Spain, and Portugal. The vows they pronounce extinguish in them forever the promptings of the flesh to which their profane fellows are subject.

CHRISM

A mixture of balm and oil. Bewitched by a bishop, it is endowed with the power of calling down the divine grace and of greasing any Christian hide that may have become too hard.

CHRISTIAN

A good-natured, simple fellow; a true lamb of the fold, who, in the innocence of his heart, persuades himself that he firmly believes unbelievable things that his priests have told him to believe, especially those he cannot even imagine. Consequently he is convinced that three x's make fifteen, that God was made a man, that he was hanged and rose to life again, that priests cannot lie, and that all who do not believe in priests will be damned without remission.

CHRISTIANITY

A religious system attributed to Jesus Christ, but really invented by Plato, improved by St. Paul, and finally revised and corrected by the Fathers, the councils, and other interpreters of the Church. Since the foundation of this sublime creed, mankind has become better, wiser, and happier than before. From that blessed epoch the world was forever freed from all strife, dissensions, troubles, vices, and evils of every kind, an invincible proof that Christianity is divine, and that it is to be possessed of the very devil himself to dare to combat such a creed or doubt its origin.

CHRONOLOGY

The Holy Spirit has fixed in Scripture the precise period of the creation of the world, but the Holy Spirit contradicts himself on this head when he speaks in Hebrew, in Greek, or in Latin. This he does with premeditation, to exercise our faith, and to amuse Messrs. Souciet and Newton.

CHURCH

In other words, the clergy. Now, this same clergy is the spouse of Christ. It is she who wears the breeches; her husband being a good-natured, easy-going fellow who, for the sake of peace, never interferes with her or contradicts her in anything. And, to tell the truth, the good lady is not easy to manage, for sometimes she treats those of her children who rebel with so much harshness as would cause her spouse to remonstrate, could he have his say in the matter.

CIRCUMCISION

The Most High, as we all know, is subject to whimsical fancies now and then, and so it happened that once upon a time he required that all his friends should pare off their foreskins. His own son submitted to this delectable ceremony. Since then, however, his papa has softened somewhat, and no longer lays claim to the foreskins of his friends, but only requires that they shall never use them.

CLERGY

The first and most important of all corporations in any well policied state. They are destined by God himself to the fulfilling of the noblest and most excellent functions, which chiefly consist in chanting, selling songs, and demanding a very high price for their celestial harmonies. The word clergy signifies inheritance or portion. If the clergy are so rich, it is simply because they are the heirs of Jesus Christ, who left, as we all know, a very large estate.

CLERGYMAN

A generic title under which is designated any Christian who consecrates himself to the service of God, or who feels himself called upon to live without working at the expense of the rascals who work to live.

CLOUDS

We can see anything we like in them, but especially signs and tokens of warfare when the priesthood is wrathy. Clouds are like holy writ, in which theologians cause the faithful or the crazy to see anything they please.

COADJUTORS

When a bishop — who, in the eyes of miscreants, seems to have little or nothing to do — bows down beneath the weight of the arduous functions of his holy ministry, a coadjutor is given him to aid and relieve him, and then the flock are in the enjoyment of two shepherds instead of one, and consequently so well guarded that the devil dares no longer prowl around the fold.

COMEDIANS

Folks who pursue an abominable calling, and who, for good reasons, are highly displeasing in the sight of the ministers of the Lord. They are proscribed and excommunicated in France, a most Christian country, where priests possess, by divine right, the exclusive privilege of acting plays.

COMMENTATORS

Learned doctors who, by dint of torturing their brains, once in a while contrive to make the words of holy writ agree with common sense, or devise ways of enunciating them in such shape as to lighten the burden of faith.

COMMERCE

Is forbidden priests and monks, who may, however, deal in certain rare and costly goods which they import from the other world. The profits they derive in France from this trade hardly attain the sum of one hundred million per year. Jesus Christ erewhile drove the merchants from the temple; these latter were, to judge from appearances, laymen traders, to whom he wished to make known the fact that the ministers of God alone have the right of turning his house into a bazaar.

COMMUNION

A spiritual banquet, at which is served a light sort of food fitted for the nourishment of pious Christian souls, but very heavy on the stomachs of such as are wanting in faith.

COMPANY (of Jesus)

A company of spiritual grenadiers of which Jesus Christ is captain. They create disturbance wherever they go, and are much more favorably inclined to little boys than they are to women.

COMPULSION

A most polite and pressing form of appeal to all who are wanting in faith, invented and made fashionable by Christianity. It compels us to enter or re-enter into the ways of salvation by imprisonment, tortures, and even cannon-balls when these latter happen to be handy.

CONCLAVE

A place in which assemble the cardinals of the most holy Catholic Church whenever there is question of electing an infallible vicar of Jesus Christ. The Holy Spirit never fails to be present at these gatherings, which is probably the reason why conclaves have never been known to make a doubtful choice.

CONCORD

Reigns ever in the midst of Christians, and especially in the midst of their theologians. The most irrefragable proof of the divine origin of Christianity is the unalterable concord that subsists among its followers, which is a miracle that confounds the human reason.

CONCORDAT

An agreement come to between a pope and a most Christian king, by which both one and the other dispose of things to which they never had the slightest claim.

CONCUPISCENCE

This word, which may sound immodest and indecent to delicate ears, is, nevertheless, a theological word, and therefore can have nothing indecent attached to it. It means that cursed attraction that, since Adam's fall, men have yielded to for all that is capable of gratifying them or giving them pleasure.

CONFESSION (auricular)

An invention very profitable to the faithful and convenient to the priests of the Romish Church. By its means they make themselves acquainted with family secrets, extort money from the timorous, engender domestic quarrels, and, if necessary, light up the flames of holy revolutions. The Church is deprived of the greater portion of the above-named advantages in countries where the people refuse to confess.

CONFESSOR

A priest who has received powers from a bishop, that is to say, to whom God himself has transmitted a power of attorney in good form, to listen to the peccadilloes which, in spite of his omniscience, God requires should be unfolded to him, without which he would not know what to think about the conscience of him or her who is confessing to the minister.

CONFIRMATION

A sacrament or holy ceremony which consists in smearing the forehead and boxing the ears of a young rogue, thereby, it is supposed, rendering him evermore firm as adamant in the faith.

CONSCIENCE

Is the judgment that we bear within ourselves of our own actions. With the profane, conscience is guided by reason; with the Christian it is regulated by faith, zeal, and the submission that is due to our reverend pastors. Consequently the conscience of a believer must often compel him to malice — even to the overthrow of society, if need be.

CONSECRATION

A series of magical words by the help of which a Romish priest has the power of compelling the God of the universe to quit his own breakfast and come down and be changed into bread himself to break the fast of the faithful.

CONSOLATIONS

The Christian religion has provided infinite consolations for her children. She consoles them for the ills and tribulations of this perishable life by teaching them that their God is a God of goodness, who chastises them for their greater good here below, and, by the effect of his divine love, may take a whim to roast them brown in the next world, which must be a very consoling thought for chilly persons.

CONTEMPLATION

A most profitable and pious occupation for those who have nothing else to do. It is clear that nothing could be more agreeable to God than the pious reveries of his elect, and that human society at large draws the greatest profit and advantages from the same.

CONTRITION

A theological term which signifies the regret felt by a Christian for the sins he has committed, with an eye to the chastisement that may follow them. This regret, according to the Jesuits, suffices to appease God, but the Jansenists deny this. God himself will doubtless some day show us which of these is right.

CONTROVERSIES

Important bickerings on contested subjects between theologians of different sects. Carnal men regard such disputes as trifles quite unworthy of occupying the attention of intelligent animals. In reality, all such quarrels are most useful to the Church militant to give her breathing time and to keep alive the fire of holy animosities, that bring so much honor and profit to the clergy.

CONVENT

A holy place within which are confined, under lock and key, any number of volumes of commentaries, syllogisms, casuistry, and theology.

CONVERSIONS

A miraculous change in the human heart due to the grace of the Most High, but of which society here below usually reaps the fruits. Conversion compels an old coquette to abandon her rouge pot, transforms an amiable and lovely woman into a vixen, changes a gentleman and a man of the world into a solemn owl, and finally induces a financier, on his deathbed, to bequeath all his possessions to the Church for the repose of his own soul and the salvation of the souls of those he has despoiled, in sheer despair

Pocket Theology   37

at not being able to take with him into the tomb the fruits of his robberies and rapine.

CORDELIERS (grey friars)

Mendicant friars who for five hundred years have edified the Church of God by their temperance, their chastity, and their fine speeches. They possess nothing of their own, their soup itself, as it is well known, belonging to his holiness the pope.

CORRECTION (fraternal)

In the Christian religion, each one should meddle with the conscience of his neighbor and take a lively interest in the salvation of his (his neighbor's) soul; should reprimand him for his faults; but, above all, should endeavor to make him renounce his errors. If he shows not a proper docility with regard to such efforts, then he should be hated and shunned, or tortured and murdered, if might be on the Christian's side.

COUNCILS

Solemn gatherings of bishops, assembled together to concert with the Holy Spirit (who is ever on the side of the stronger) touching the dogmas and all necessary arrangements of the Church. Councils are necessary to correct, explain, and alter the holy scripture and the accepted doctrine, and to fix for the time being the articles of faith, without which the human race would be damned.

COURT

Were it not for kingly courts, little prosperity could be hoped for by the Church and the Holy Ghost would be docked of one wing.

It is in these that all questions of orthodoxy are decided finally and without appeal. Heretics are those whose opinions do not side with those of a court. The divinities here below usually govern the destinies of the divinities above. Had it not been for Constantine, Jesus Christ would have been of little or no account on the earth.

COWL

A piece of woolen stuff designed to cover the nape of the neck and the science contained in a friar's noddle. The form of this sacred gew-gaw has been the pretext for some of the bloodiest dissensions in the Church, resulting in the burning at the stake of several hundred cowled monks.

CREATION

An inconceivable act of the Almighty, who, out of nothing, has made all that our eyes can contemplate. Atheists deny the possibility of the fact, but these are wanting in faith. Theologians are daily proving to us that the least thing in the world would suffice to set the globe on fire. The Church is daily proving to us that out of nothing she can coin gold and silver, and it is incontestable that her priests divide with the Most High the power of creating, for is it not well known that the priest Needham recently created eels?

CREDIBILITY

According to theologians, motives of credibility are convincing reasons or plain proofs that compel us to believe any given thing. In religion, the motives that compel us to believe are the word of our pastor, ignorance, customs, but above all and before all, the fear of getting ourselves into trouble.

CREDULITY

All pious Christians should cultivate that happy simplicity of the heart which disposes them to credit the most incredible things on the authority of their spiritual guides. These latter are of course incapable of deceiving themselves, and much less of deceiving others.

CRIMES

In religion this term does not mean actions hurtful to society at large, but actions that are hurtful to the clergy. The greatest of all crimes is to be wanting in faith and in trust in that body, to question its opinions, to rob its churches, and to disdain its holy things. All and each of these crimes are punishable with fire in this world or the next.

CROSIER

The augural staff of the ancient Romans, which, in certain ceremonies of the more modern Romish church, is borne by the bishops and the privileged abbots. It is a symbol and a sign to all good Christians that they are but sheep and have nothing better to do than allow themselves to be shorn by these reverend shepherds.

CROSS

The sign and standard of salvation. It is composed of two staves of wood, crossed, and represents the gibbet upon which the Godhead was hanged. Servants of the Lord, like brother John of Automures, use it to chatise rogues who pillage their orchards. To bear one's cross is to fret and worry one's self with pious peevishness, to worry and torment ourselves when we have nothing else to do, and to worry and torment our neighbors to the end that they may the more surely obtain the kingdom of heaven.

CRUELTY

A troublesome disposition for the conduct of the affairs of everyday life, but very necessary for the maintenance of the faith. Humanity is out of season when either the divinity or his divine ministers are in question.

CRUSADES

Pious expeditions ordained by the popes to clear Europe of a multitude of villainous bigots, who, to obtain from heaven the remission of the crimes they had committed at home, went valiantly and committed others against their neighbors.

CURIOSITY

An exceedingly great sin. God once condemned to death the whole human race for the sin of curiosity on the part of a woman who wanted to know the difference between good and evil; which proves that he is highly displeased with us if we happen to have a little common sense or may desire to know anything that it pleases his ministers we should not know.

DAMNATION

We are bound to believe, under pain of being damned, that the God of all mercy, to teach sinners how to live after their death, and to chastise those that are living who are blind, damns to all eternity the greater portion of mankind for venial faults, and that by a special miracle of his divine love he causes them to endure everlastingly that he may everlastingly torture them. The Church, like God, has the right to damn. There are even those who believe that, were it not for the Church, the Most High would damn nobody, and that he only does so to cheer and enliven his spouse.

DATARY'S OFFICE

A sacred office in Rome, where, for payment, are distributed benefices, dispensations, and graces of the Holy Ghost, and even the right of committing sins.

DAVID

One of the greatest saints in heaven, and a real pattern for kings. A rebel, a rake, and an adulterer, he lay with the wives and murdered the husbands, but was withal very pious and submissive to the priests, for which reasons they proclaimed him to be a man after God's own heart. God himself, even in these days, is never better pleased than when hearing repeated to him the vaudevilles composed by this most holy man.

DEATH

Is the penalty of sin, but had it not been for the sin of Adam, the human race would not die, trees would not die, dogs would not die. All trees have sinned in the person of the tree which bore the forbidden fruit; all brutes have sinned in the person of the serpent that beguiled Eve; all men have sinned in the person of Adam, and this is why all men, all brutes, and all plants are subject to death. Let us take comfort, however; for to all Christians death is but the entrance into life, and moreover procures a good living for our sacrificers, who contrive to make as much profit out of the dead as the living. The stench of a corpse has the strongest attractions for reverend crows and pious cormorants.

DEICIDE

A crime committed by the Jews when they put to death a God whom they had not wit enough to discover under the form of a red-headed Jew, who thus deceived them to the end of punishing them afterwards for having been deceived.

DEISM

An impious system, which supports a too reasonable God, who requires nothing more of men than that they shall be good and true, and asks from them neither faith nor worship nor vain ceremonies. It is evident that such a system is absurd and in no manner suitable for the clergy; a like religion could have no need of priests, which would be most damaging to theology.

DELUGE

A paternal chastisement inflicted on the human race by Divine Providence, who, through not having foreseen the malice and wickedness of men, repented of having made them, and drowned them once for all to make them better — an act which, as we all know, was attended with the greatest success.

DEPOSITION

Bishops alone have the right of judging and deposing a bishop. No sovereign, without being guilty of sacrilege, can exercise such right. From the time when Samuel deposed King Saul, bishops have enjoyed the right of deposing kings; whence it will be seen that it was quite legally that the bishops deposed Louis the Good at the Council of Soissons, and that the pope has a right to depose kings.

DEVIL

The black sheep of the heavenly hosts, and the main prop of the Church. God, with a single word, could annihilate him, but is very careful not to do so; he stands too much in need of him himself for his own purposes, and therefore leaves him at large, and endures patiently all the tricks he is daily and hourly playing upon him, his wife, and his children. Without the devil, God would cut but a sorry figure at best. The love of God is frequently but the fear of the devil, and without that fear it might happen that a goodly number of the devout would never think of God or his priests at all.

DEVOTION

A pious devotedness to priests, or a holy exactitude in fulfilling the duties laid down by them. Devout people — in other words, Christians — being duly permeated and imbued with these elevated sentiments, have the advantage of being flat, wearisome, insipid, unsociable, and therefore fit to be taken to the realms above with the greatest possible dispatch. Female devotees are pious prudes, who work most efficaciously for the salvation of all who approach them by inspiring them with holy disgust for them and all their surroundings.

DIGNITARIES

Worldly titles awarded by the religion of the God of humility to his humble ministers who no longer think fit to remain in the poverty stricken condition in which he himself remained during his stay here below.

DIRECTOR

A holy, stiff-necked man, withal generally gluttonous, whose functions are to introduce himself into the bosom of families to the end of exciting domestic quarrels, getting the children and the servants reprimanded, and turning crazy the brains of his devotees, the surer to guide them in the ways of salvation.

DISCIPLINE

Salutary rules and arrangements which the ministers of God judge suitable to their interests, and which they change at will in conformity with the immutable decrees of the Godhead. This word also designates an instrument of cord or wire, which does great good to the soul when applied to the body.

DISPENSATION

A permission to do evil accorded by the pope or the bishops for payment in hard cash. By virtue of such dispensation what was before illegal and criminal becomes legal and sinless, seeing that the products of the sale go to increase the funds in the cash-box of the Eternal Father & Co.

DISPUTES

Interesting and edifying debates that frequently arise among the infallible interpreters of the word of God, who, for the greater good of his church, has not judged it expedient too express himself too explicitly for fear his dear ministers should then have nothing to quarrel about.

DIVORCE

Is absolutely forbidden to Catholic Christians, with whom marriage is indissoluble. The result is, of course, highly beneficial to certain married couples who cannot agree, for thus they are enabled to torment each other for the whole length of their lives, and to obtain the kingdom of heaven. Divorce is only permitted to bishops, who may at their pleasure exchange a poor and homely wife for a rich and pretty one.

DOCTRINE

What every good Christian must believe, under pain of being burnt either in this world or the next. The dogmas of religion are the immutable decrees of God, and cannot change except when the Church changes them.

DOMINANT

The dominant religion is that of a prince who, with the help of fire and sword, proves incontrovertibly to the other religions of his kingdom that they are wrong and that his confessor is right, and that it is his (the prince's) councils that must regulate creed or faith.

DOMINATION (spirit of)

Ambition, or the desire to domineer, is happily a passion quite foreign to the breasts of the ministers of the gospel; their empire is not of this world; it is wholly spiritual; content with their rule over the mind, they have no fear that the body, which is but the sheath of the mind, will ever refuse to bend to their sacred will.

DONATIONS

Presents which the Church, in her kindness for her children, consents to receive from the profane. All that is given to God belongs to the clergy. *Daleunt Domino et exit sacerdotis.*

DRAGOONS

Most orthodox missionaries sent by the court of Versailles to the Huguenots (French Protestants) to argue with them on transubstantiation, to lead them back to the bosom of the Church, and to prove to them that the pope is the confessor of the king, and cannot err.

DUTIES

Duties, in religion, are those that are founded on the relations that exist between men and their priests, and it is therefore the priests alone who can claim to define the duties of a good Christian. These consist in praying long and fervently, in listening to what they do not understand, and, above all, in paying with a generous hand the ministers of the Lord.

DYING (the)

If the dying have ceased to be of much account to society in general, they are of very much account still to the Church in particular, who causes them to give with a liberal hand that which they cannot take with them. It is beside the deathbed that the priest is in his glory; at such moments it sometimes happens that even Infidels acknowledge their errors and give in to arguments that fear and weakness of body and mind cause them to regard as unanswerable. The truths of religion are never so well understood as by those who have lost the power of reasoning. He need care for nothing else. It is beside the bed of the dying that sacerdotal stoicism shines with its purest rays.

EARS

Organs with which a good Christian should be well provided, seeing that faith enters into us through the ears, "fides ex auditu" as St. Paul says. (See Asses, Education, Parrots.)

EASTER

A solemn feast clandestinely celebrated by Christians in remembrance of the resurrection of a God who was publicly hanged. To the end of celebrating this great day with all due honor, the Christians eat their God, doubtless to ascertain if, like the Phoenix, he will spring into new life from that which has devoured him. Once upon a time the members of the Church of God engaged together in hot dispute touching the precise period of the year at which the feast of Easter should be celebrated. A most grave and reverend council decided that the equinoctial moon of spring should regulate this important piece of business, a fact which clearly demonstrates that the Church, like the rest of her sex, is "subject to the changes of the moon."

ECSTACY

A holy state of syncope, during which pious persons are allowed to dream dreams and see visions. Persons who are subject to falling into such a state are as a rule either rogues or fools, and sometimes a happy mixture of both.

EDIFICATION

To edify a person is to fortify in him by precept and example the pious respect he should entertain for religious things and the worth of God's ministers. With regard to the latter, they are always edifying, everywhere, but especially in Spain and Italy, and are especially respected there in consequence.

EDUCATION (Christian)

Consists in training small Christians, from their earliest infancy, in the healthful habits of making as little use of their reason as may be, of believing all they are told to believe, of hating all who do not believe what they believe — all to the end of raising up for the state sensible and reasoning citizens, orderly fearing God, and above all humbly submissive to the clergy.

ELECT

The elect are those whom God in his mercy has chosen to be heirs to the kingdom of heaven. Each succeeding century provides about half a dozen or so of these elect, who shall enjoy the ineffable satisfaction of seeing the rest of mankind consuming in eternal flames.

ENTHUSIASM

A species of holy drunkenness which seizes on the brain of those who by God's grace have imbibed large doses of the excellent wine sold by the priests in their sacred taverns.

ERROR

In matters of religion, any way of thinking that differs from the way of thinking of the priests, in whom we should have all trust. With the Christians, there is not a more unpardonable crime than to be in error, and such crime is righteously punished with the greatest rigor. Nothing less than fire can efficaciously enlighten and lead back into the path of duty he who is stupid enough to wander away from it.

ETERNITY

That which has neither beginning nor end. As this is more easy to say than to understand, all good Christians will do well to meditate upon it with the help of their ministers, who will not fail to make it clear to them. In the meanwhile, under pain of being roasted, and in spite of the preacher *Petit Pierre* hold for sure and certain that the pains of hell are eternal. Jesus Christ never said so, but the Church, which goes much farther than he, has said so, and is ever saying so, for the greater consolation of her dear children, ninety-nine of whom at least out of every hundred will be damned.

EUCHARIST

A wonderful sacrament, in which the God of the universe is good enough to allow himself to be eaten by his priests and such good Christians as have stomachs strong enough to digest him.

EUNUCH

It would be well for the interests of the Church if all were made eunuchs; as then the world would soon come to an end, and God would be no longer offended by mankind.

EVIL

Came into the world through the sin of Adam. If that idiot had not sinned, we should not have been afflicted with the small pox, nor the itch, nor theology, nor the faith which alone can save us.

EXCOMMUNICATION

A spiritual penalty imposed by the shepherds of the Church on those of its sheep who are mangy. In other times this penalty caused to wither up and be stricken with sudden death divers princes and great ones of the earth, but in these latter days its effects are not by any means so marked; which proves that faith is daily decreasing and becoming more rare here below.

EXERCISES (pious)

Certain nice little spiritual occupations invented by the priests to stir up and keep awake the drowsy souls of devout Christians, and in default of which said devout Christians might run the risk of doing something useful either to their families or to a wicked world. Divers movements of the lips, the ears, and the body, without which a man cannot render himself agreeable in the eyes of God nor of his priests. Devotional exercises, which may appear odd, nay grotesque, to the eye of an unbeliever, are not so in the eyes of the clergy, because, in the first place, they are profitable, and in the second, they accustom believers to obey without reasoning or question.

EXAMINATION

It is a great sin for a good Catholic to presume to examine whatever is said by his self-proclaimed infallible clergy. Good Protestants, on the other hand, may examine whatever is said by their clergy, which does not proclaim itself infallible, provided they be of the same way of thinking as the clergy.

EXORCISM

An act of authority exclusively exercised by the priests of the Romish Church, and which, by dint of holy water, speeches, and ceremonies, drives devils out of bodies into which they had never entered, or only entered into for a financial consideration.

EXPIATION

Means here to liquidate a debt or debts contracted towards God, and consists in certain ceremonies invented by the priests, the solicitors and legal advisers of the Most High. At the request of the former the latter cancels all debts that are owing him, provided the legal fees be paid.

EYES

Organs of the body very useful to all good Christians, who should shut them the better to advance in the way of salvation; nay, should even tear them out should the clergy scandalize them.

EXTREME UNCTION

A most venerable sacrament of the Romish Church, and very efficacious in frightening the dying. It consists principally in greasing the brogans of all who are departing on the journey to another world.

EZEKIEL

A great prophet of Judea, celebrated for the visions he saw and the excellent lunches he sat down to. Our modern prophets, it were needless to say, do not envy him the latter. He is assuredly, with the exception of the Jesuit Sanchez and the janitor of the convent of the Chartreuse, the most smutty priest that was ever known.

FABLES

All the tales and legends told by all the religions of the earth are but fables, a goodly number of them being, moreover, of the dullest and most monotonous description. Those to be found in the Bible are alone authentic, and he who does not wish to be thrown into an everlasting boiling cauldron must regard them as true.

FAITH

A pious trust in priests, who make us believe whatever they tell us, even though we may not understand it. It is the first of Christian virtues, and is theological that is to say, useful to theologians. Without it there can be no religion, and, consequently, no salvation. Its chief effects are to plunge us into and keep us in a state of pious torpor, accompanied by a holy obstinacy and a profound disdain for human reason and common sense. This virtue is most profitable to the Church, and is a gift of divine grace, induced by a habit of raving perpetually, or the fear of getting one's self into trouble. Thus it follows that all those who have not been endowed with this grace, or who have not had the opportunity of contracting this pious custom, are of no mortal use to the Church, and consequently only fit for the dunghill.

FAITHFUL (the)

All pious Christians who are devoutly attached to God and his priests in defiance of all and everything. The faithful, as we know, owe allegiance to princes only in proportion as the latter show themselves submissive to the Church, that is to say, to her ministers.

FAMILIARS

A name given in Spain and in Portugal to certain distinguished noblemen who, in their humility, made themselves the spies, the informers, and the alguazils of the most holy Inquisition.

FANATICISM

A holy rage or sacred contagion proper to Christianity. It specially effects all good Christians of heated blood and zealous brain. It is contracted through the ear, and resists alike common sense and violent remedies. Broths, wines, and asylums for the insane are its most reliable specifics.

FASTING

Means to abstain from taking food, a pious practice most agreeable to God, who only gave us stomachs and aliments that we might die of starvation. When we cannot fast ourselves, we should make some one else fast for us. One of the many advantages derived from fasting is that it disposes us most efficaciously to see anything the priests desire we should see on an empty stomach. St. Bernard tells us that while the body is fasting, the soul fares sumptuously, and becomes as fat as a sucking pig. The

Greek and Latin Christians are convinced that the Almighty, like a custom-house officer, examines attentively, from his celestial dormer-window all the provisions that enter into the stomachs of his elect. He does not think, of course, that during his holy Lent the latter would introduce into the former such food as turkey, chicken, and mutton, but is well pleased, nevertheless, that they content themselves with herrings, codfish, eels, and eggs, which the archbishops kindly permit.

FATALITY

A horrible system, which submits all and everything to necessity in a universe governed by the immutable laws of the Almighty, without whose will nothing can happen. If all things are ruled by the law of necessity, then good-bye to man's free will, of which the priests stand so much in need to be able to damn him.

FATHERS OF THE CHURCH

Holy visionaries who have provided the Church with any number of dialecticians, dogmas, and wise interpolations, from whom and which the Church does not allow us to appeal to common sense.

FEAR

Is the beginning of wisdom. Men never reason so excellently as when they are very much frightened. Of all people, poltroons are the most useful to the cause of religion. If ever the human race forgets its cowardice, so surely will the priests remember theirs.

FIGURES

Types, allegories, an obscure manner of expressing himself very common with the Holy Spirit, who, it would appear, has never yet been able to persuade himself to speak in plain language to those whom he would enlighten, and this for no other reason than to provide for the doctors of the Church divers opportunities to show their astonishing sagacity.

FILIAL

A filial fear mixed with love should be felt by all good Christians for a God who is not always in the best of tempers, and for the Holy Church, his spouse, who frequently shows herself to be a virago and a shrew.

FINANCIERS

The publicans of the New Testament. With the one exception of the treasurer of the clergy, they will all be damned, unless, indeed, some charitable priests should rid them of a portion of the mammon of iniquity.

FINGER OF GOD

Whenever any important event, a revolution, or a calamity turns to the profit of the Church, such is always signalized as the finger of God, who never loses sight of his good friends, the clergy, save and except on the rare occasions when Satan in his turn raps the knuckles of said finger.

FIRE

The Christian religion is essentially a religion of fire. Christians should ever burn with divine love, priests should ever burn incense, the hangman should ever burn forbidden books in the marketplace, and princes and magistrates should ever burn heretics, Atheists, and other miscreants.

FLAGELLATIONS

Pious and salutary scourgings, self-administered by Christians who aim at perfection, to the end of mortifying the flesh, quickening the spirit, and giving some occasion for fun to the Eternal Father of all, who laughs in his divine sleeve every time he it shown a well-chastised pair of shoulders or a thoroughly "whaled" posterior.

FLESH (the)

Is ever opposed to the spirit, and must be mortified. This recipe is eminently calculated to insure a cheerful spirit.

FOLLY

All good Christians glory in the folly of the cross. Nothing can be more contrary to religion and the clergy than reason and common sense. These will not accept faith, nor are they susceptible of either fervor or zeal. Mohammedans show respect to fools or madmen, and with regard to Christians, assuredly their greatest and most venerable saints were those whose brains had sustained the severest shock.

FOOLS

Unbelievers, who are fools, can see with their profane eyes nothing but fools and foolishness in our holy religion; they see therein but a foolish God, who foolishly allowed himself to be hanged, foolish apostles, foolish mysteries, foolish opinions, foolish quarrels, foolish practices which occupy foolish people, who give a good time to the priests, who are anything but fools.

FORCE

A virtue most useful and efficacious for the maintenance of the faith and the property of the Church. It consists in priests forcing, by every means in their power, obstinate people to think as they do; with the laity it consists in vigorously repulsing all suggestions of reason and common sense and in trustfully bearing the burden of the ministers of the Lord.

FORGIVENESS OF INJURIES

Very laudable conduct in laymen, to whom it is prescribed in the gospel; priests may dispense with it and never forgive, seeing that it is not they who are offended, but God. The God of all mercy would never forgive them did they forgive those who offend him, especially in the person of his clergy. This is the sin against the Holy Ghost which shall never be forgiven, either in this world or the next. Nevertheless, the priests may forgive those whom they have caused to be massacred, provided they leave behind them neither children, parents, nor relatives who may be also lawfully massacred according to the law of the Bible.

FOUNDATIONS

Revenues granted to priests and friars so that they may eat well, drink well, sleep well, and sing well, to the end that the vineyards of those who have not the time to sing be assured against rain and hail. Hence it will be seen that it is the priests who are the sole clerks of the weather here below.

FRAUDS (pious)

Pious rogueries, religious lies, devout impostures, of which the clergy make most legitimate use to feed the faith of the vulgar and to further the good cause of injuring our enemies, against whom all weapons are lawful.

FREE WILL

Man is a free agent; were it otherwise, the priests could not damn him. Free will is a small present which God has bestowed as a signal favor on the human race. By the help of this free will we are gifted above all other animals and plants with the faculty of being able to damn ourselves to all eternity whenever our free will is not in perfect accord with the divine will of him who will thus enjoy the pleasure of punishing him whom he has allowed to anger him.

FROCK

A sacred garment reserved for monks and friars, who are men of God. By an astounding miracle the frock communicates to these the virtue of continence as soon as put on; witness the dog of M. Malinotier.

FULMINATION

The spiritual artillery of the Church. It is composed of mortars and intellectual cannon, which the heads of the Church have the right of aiming at the souls of whomsoever has the audacity to disagree with them. This metaphysical artillery likewise inflicts wounds bodily, when it is sustained by a material artillery kept in reserve by secular priests in their arsenals.

FUNERALS

Ceremonies which the ministers of the Lord render more or less dismal by their saintly howls in proportion to the pay they have received.

FUTURE

A country known to priestly geographers, where God will doubtless pay, on their falling due, all the bills that his brokers and agents have drawn on him. In no one instance has he ever permitted the bills of his business men to be protested, all such being, as is well known, payable on sight.

GHOSTS (unholy)

It should be an article of faith to believe in them. It is always as well to accustom people to be afraid of something or other; the Church can only gain by it. The devil is the bugbear that frightens children of forty years and upwards.

GIFTS (gratuitous)

By divine right the clergy owe nothing to the state. If they contribute to its needs, it is through pure condescension. They sojourn in the state solely to be protected, respected, remunerated; they do the state honor enough by honoring it with their presence, aiding it with their prayers, enlightening it with their wisdom, and relieving it of its money-bags.

GLORY OF GOD

The God of the Christians is a proud God, a very proud God, if we are to believe one-half of what his priests are constantly telling us on this subject. It is doubtless to the greater glory of God that those who represent him here on earth would now and again turn that earth topsy-tury if they could, and which, by-the-bye, they have a legitimate right to do, inasmuch as God created the earth to his own glory, which somehow or other is invariably confused and mixed up with the glory of the priests.

GOD

A word synonymous with priests, or, rather, the factotum of theologians, the principal agent of the clergy, the business man, the purveyor, the commissary of the sacred army. The word of God is the word of the priests; the glory of God is the pride of the priests; the will of God is the will of the priests. To offend God is to offend the priests; to believe in God is to believe all that the priests tell us. When God is said to be wroth, it means that the priests are out of temper. By substituting the word priest for the word God, theology becomes the simplest of sciences. This established, it follows that there can be no true Atheists, seeing that no one but a triple imbecile would attempt to deny the existence of the clergy, which is a very palpable fact. There is, of course, another and quite different God, but the priests hold him of little account. Theirs is the true one, and men must acknowledge him if they do not want to roast in the other world.

GOODNESS

Divine perfection. God is all good, without the least mixture of evil. It is true that in spite of his goodness he frequently harms us, or permits others to harm us. This, however, proves nothing, for he is invariably good to his ministers, and this ought to suffice for us.

GOOSE

There is a series of tales called the tales of Mother Goose. The tales told us by the Church are also tales of Mother Goose, seeing that we are goslings and the Church is our mother.

GOSPEL

Signifies good news. The good news that the gospel of the Christians came to announce to them is that their God is a God of wrath, that he has predestined the far greater number of them to hell-fire, that their happiness depends on their pious imbecility, their holy credulity, their sacred ravings, on the evils they do to one another through their hatred one for another, on their unintelligible meaning, on their zeal, on their antipathy for and persecution of all who do not agree with them or resemble them. Such are the good tidings that the Godhead, in its great love and tenderness for the human race, has sent down to them. Such was the joy with which the latter received the former that ever since its advent they have done nothing but weep, lament, quarrel, and fight and gnash their teeth at each other.

GRACE

A gratuitous gift which the Most High bestows on whomsoever he pleases, of course reserving to himself the right of chastising all to whom he has denied it. It has never yet been decided whether, to produce its proper effect, grace should be abundant or efficient. The recipient must therefore wait until God grants him the grace to know what grace is.

GREATNESS

The Church of God despises the greatness of this world; its ministers never so much as give it a thought; its bishops especially show a marked aversion for worldly titles, orders, honors, etc., and you could not be guilty of a greater offense toward one of their number than by calling him "Your Eminence."

HANGMAN (public)

The best of all Christians in a Christian country, and the most orthodox of its citizens. He is the friend of the priests, the defender of the faith, and, in a word, the most indispensable of all men to the priests and to the cause of God.

HARSHNESS

Harshness, or hardness of heart, has ever been more or less attributed to the members of the clergy. Such harshness is with them only the effect of the sublimest virtue. A true Christian should be wholly unfeeling. He is a perfect priest on whom God in his grace has bestowed a head of brass and a heart of steel.

HATRED

A most praiseworthy feeling, and necessary to all good Christians when their priests think fit to excite it in their bosoms for the cause of God against the unbelieving. Thus, on the faith of the word of his confessor, a devout Christian may cordially and conscientiously hate any one who disagrees with such confessor, and without in any wise wounding Christian charity.

HEAVEN

A far distant country where resides the God who fills the universe with his immensity. It is thence that our priests import, at a very slender outlay, the dogmas, arguments, and other spiritual and airy articles that they sell to the Christians. There, seated on his throne of clouds, the Most High at their behests dispenseth to the nations of the earth dews or deluges, soft rain or tempests, calamities or prosperity, and last though not least, those pious dissensions so necessary for the maintenance of the faith. There are three heavens as we are all aware. St. Paul saw the second, but has given no map of its whereabouts, a fact rather embarrassing to geographers.

HELL

A cooking-stove which heats the sacerdotal saucepan here below. It was founded in behalf of our priests, to the end that the latter may never be wanting in good cheer. Our Eternal Father, who is chief cook, makes roasts and bakes of those of his children who have not deferred sufficiently to their teachings. At the feast of the Lamb the elect shall eat of the flesh of broiled Infidels, fricasseed rich men, financiers *a la* Worcestershire sauce, etc.

HERESIES

Are necessary to the Church inasmuch as they call into play the talents, and polish and keep free from rust the swords, of her reverend gladiators. Any opinion or opinions adverse to those expressed by the theologians, in whom we have the fullest trust, or who have power or credit enough to force such trust from us, are evidently heretical. Hence it will be seen that among theologians heretics are those of their number who are not backed with a sufficient array of battalions to render them orthodox.

HETERODOX

Such are all who do not think like the orthodox, or who have not strength and might sufficient to make themselves orthodox.

HIERARCHY

The order of the divers ranks occupied by the ministers of J. C. in his father's mansion, where, however, he has told us himself, there should be neither first nor last in his eyes. His spouse, however, who understands the management of his affairs much better than he does himself, has ordered things otherwise — so much so, indeed, that there is now in the divine family as great a distance from a bishop to a curate as there is from God the Father to St. Crispin, who was but a cobbler of Soissons.

HISTORY (ecclesiastical)

A study most necessary to churchmen, but very injurious to laymen, whose faith might not always be sufficiently robust not to be scandalized by the pious deportment of the ministers of the Lord.

HOLIDAYS

Certain days wisely set apart by the Church to be spent in holy idleness, which is favorable to piety. An artisan may not, without sin, work for his bread on a holiday though he may get drunk if he chooses and has the means of doing so. However, the safest manner of passing such days is to sit and yawn your head off.

HOLOCAUSTS

Victims either roasted or broiled, or both, offered up as a sacrifice. The divinity would seem to have ever had a most pronounced taste for roasts, seeing the high esteem in which his priests have ever held such.

HOLY SCRIPTURE

A book sent down from heaven for the express purpose that the clergy may find therein all that they want to find. Holy scripture contains all that a Christian should know and believe, provided he adds to it a million or so of commentaries.

HOLY SPIRIT

The conscience of the gods who compose the sole God of the Christians. His functions are to inspire the priests and to be in their midst whenever so required. In the eyes of carnal men the Holy Spirit shows but a very moderate amount of spirit.

HOLY WATER

Is called lustral water by the pagans, but priests render it most holy, most Christian, and most efficacious by the aid of certain incantations to be found in certain old conjuring books called rituals.

HOPE

A Christian virtue which consists in our despising all poor things here below in the expectation of enjoying in an unknown country unknown joys which our priests promise us for the worth of our money.

HOSPITALS

Pious institutions in favor of the poor; that is to say, of those who manage and direct them. God rewards them, even in this life, for their tender care of those confided to their charge. The managers and directors of these institutions are usually well housed, clad in purple and fine linen, and fare sumptuously every day.

HUMANITY

A virtue of profane ethics which all good Christians should stifle in their bosoms as it seldom or ever accords with the interests of the Divinity, with whom, in conjunction with humanity, the priests would fare but poorly. For the rest, God's ministers are always so busy with the management of heavenly affairs that they have very little time to devote to the interests of mankind. But although the priests have no humanity themselves, they nevertheless cause us to go through our humanities by making us learn a little bad Latin and a great deal of catechism.

HUMILITY

A Christian virtue which prepares the way for faith. It is a virtue specially useful to the ministers of the Gospel, to whose lights it is of the greatest importance we should defer. It chiefly consists in a contempt for one's self and a fear of incurring the esteem of one's neighbor, whence it arises that it is one of the virtues the most fitted to the molding of great men. In the Church of God, all breathes of humility, all teaches humility; the bishops are humble; the Jesuits are humble; a cardinal does not esteem himself higher than the janitor of a Capuchin convent, and the Pope most humbly places himself above all kings of the earth, and said kings are most subservient to this doorkeeper of Paradise.

HYPOCRISY

An easy way of getting on in life by getting the clergy on our side. All hypocrites are therefore of great help to the cause of God, defending it as they generally do with much more zeal than sincerely devout people, who are frequently rather obtuse and simple.

IDEAS (innate)

Thus are called certain notions instilled into our minds so earnestly and so persistently by our nurses and our priests that when we have grown to be men and women we imagine we received them even in our mother's womb. All ideas set forth in the catechism are clearly innate ideas.

IDLENESS

Is the mother of all the vices. If there were no priests in the world, people would not have work enough to do, and would become loafers and tramps. If priests consecrate themselves to idleness, it is for no other reason than to diminish the number of the vices of the laity, who are thus obliged to labor, not only for themselves, but for the mighty army of the Lord's lazy-bones.

IDOLATRY

Religious worship rendered to material and inanimate objects. Our worship is due to the only true God, and cannot, therefore, be transferred to any of his creatures without sin, unless, indeed, the only true God should take a fancy to turn himself into a wafer, or to change a wafer into himself, which, of course, would make it quite a different thing altogether.

IGNORANCE

Is the opposite of knowledge and the first step to faith, and of the highest importance to the Church, seeing that since the laity has become more enlightened, faith has declined on the earth, the heart of charity has become hardened, and the shares of the priesthood are hourly rendering more modest dividends.

IMITATION

The Christian religion commands us to imitate the God we adore, whence we must infer that it is our duty to lay snares for the feet of men and then punish them for having fallen into them; to persecute and exterminate Infidels, to send sinners to the devil, and finally to get ourselves gibbeted to complete the resemblance between ourselves and our divine model.

IMMATERIAL

That which is not material, or that which is spiritual. If you desire any further explanation on this head, apply to your priest, who will prove to you that God is immaterial, that your soul is immaterial, and that your understanding, being too material, understands nothing. Let faith attend you, or dread that on a day to come your obtuse spirit be materially or spiritually roasted for having been too material.

IMMENSE

God is immense; his presence fills all space; he is everywhere. Then he is within me when I sin or act unwisely! Nothing of the sort, you idiot; he can be everywhere without being in you — don't you see? H'm I Ha! A mystery. Oh, yes; now I understand!

IMMORTALITY

A quality proper to our soul, which, as we know, is a spirit. Now, a spirit is a substance of the nature of which we have no knowledge, and it cannot, therefore, be destroyed by the same elements as the substances we have a knowledge of. It is most essential to the Church that our souls should be immortal, for otherwise the ministers of the Church might be obliged to go into bankruptcy.

IMMUTABLE

God is immutable, or, in other words, not susceptible of change. Nevertheless, we find among his letters and papers that he has frequently changed his projects, his friends, and even his religion; all these changes are of course without prejudice to his immutability or to that of his immutable priests, who are unchanging and steadfast in their purpose of leading laymen by the nose to the end of all time.

IMMUNITIES

Privileges most wisely granted by princes, or rather by the Godhead himself to his valets and footmen. In virtue of such immunities, the latter may be as arrogant and insolent as they please, and are dispensed from contributing like other men to the needs and wants of the human society. God is never so wroth as when a sacrilegious hand lays itself on the immunities of his domestics, and always punishes such an act by the most terrible chastisement.

IMPECCABILITY

God himself has promised to his Church that she shall ever remain lovely and lovable, that she shall inherit immortal youth, that she shall never mouth and rave, and that the gates of hell shall not prevail against her. However, in spite of these assurances, she hits out right and left, and raises the deuce generally if a word be spoken that does not sound agreeable to her ears. This manner of being on her part proceeds less from a want of faith than from the fear of a possible failing of funds, which serve to keep bright the face of youth.

IMPENITENCE

A hardening in sin. If a soul persevere even unto death in its revolt against God and his Church, then impenitence is called forth. It is the most deadly of all sins in the eyes of the clergy, who could never consent that God should condone it.

IMPIOUS (the)

People who are not pious, or, being wanting in faith, have the impertinence to laugh at things which the truly devout and the priests have agreed among themselves are grave and sacred. An impious woman is one who is not a magpie like her servant, sister, or her prudish aunt.

IMPIETY

All that is injurious and detrimental to the honor of God, that is to say, of the clergy.

IMPLICIT

The distinguishing character of a well-conditioned faith, that is, of a faith that causes us to believe all the priests tell us if we are Catholics; all that Prof. Vernet says if we are natives of Geneva; and all that the mufti says if we are inhabitants of Constantinople.

INCEST

Was a sin against nature in the days of Adam, but has been and is still sanctioned by the popes, if they are paid a good price for such a sanction. To lie with one's godmother is spiritual incest, and quite as bad as corporeal incest, and will be punished in like manner.

INCOMPREHENSIBLE

God is incomprehensible, as are likewise the mysteries of his Church. The priests alone are able to comprehend both one and the other, a fact to be ascribed to the remarkable formation and capacity of the priestly brain.

INCREDULOUS (the)

Any number of rogues who are not credulous, and who have the impertinence to think that it might just happen that God has not said all that has been put into his mouth, and that his priests may have kept back things that he has said. It is plain that such individuals are quite useless to the clergy, and consequently useless to society, which cannot do without the clergy. Moreover, has not St. Augustine declared that the sin of incredulity is the greatest of all sins?

INDULGENCES

Spiritual graces granted by God or the pope to the faithful, and which have for effect to remit their sins in the past and the future. Indulgences must not be confounded with what the profane call indulgence, the clergy having neither the right nor the desire to pretend to anything of that sort.

INFALLIBILITY

An exclusive privilege granted by God himself to his Church. The bishops assembled in council cannot err on questions of faith, if they have power and influence enough to have their decisions passed and approved of. Some Christians believe that the pope is infallible, but others, again, have the courage to entertain and to express grave doubts on that head. It may be accepted, as a general rule, that every bishop, priest, preacher, rabbi, iman, etc., is infallible as long as there is danger in contradicting him.

IMPORTANT

There is nothing so important in the whole world as that which it imports the priests to cause to be regarded as important. The Christian world has had for some centuries past the happiness of being constantly troubled and thrown into strife and turmoil about certain important words, important arguments, important epochs, important ceremonies, important bulls, etc.

IMPOSITION (of hands)

A holy ceremony necessary to the making of a priest, and not of an impostor, as the word itself would seem to imply. This holy act draws down the Holy Spirit on the pate of a priest, who therefore can never lie again, and will always speak the truth, provided, however, that whatever he says be approved by his bishop, who, as we all know, got *his* faith at the fountain-head.

INCARNATION

Every good Christian is bound to believe that he who fills the universe with his immensity, once upon a time made himself so small as to be able to enter into the hide of a Jew. He had but slight reason to congratulate himself on the metamorphosis, however, and it is hardly likely that he will try it again.

INFANCY

A state of helplessness, ignorance, and imbecility, in which it is necessary to maintain Christians, to the end of enabling their priests the more easily to lead them to heaven, from which they would inevitably be excluded if they were grown enough to be able to walk without leading strings.

INFINITE

That which is not finished or has no end. God is infinite; that is to say, the theologians are not very exactly informed as to the extent of his attributes. The clergy partake of the infinite with God, as they are, like him, infinitely wise, infinitely powerful, infinitely respected by the Christians in their infinite simplicity of head and heart.

INFORMATION

The Christian religion, being the upholder of society and the stronghold of all the virtues, maintains in its midst spies and informers, turns children against their parents, servants against their masters, and *vice versa*, a state of things which renders the relations of life both secure and agreeable to all parties.

INGRATITUDE

An odious disposition of the mind in laymen, who should never lose sight of their immense obligations to the clergy; the clergy may be ungrateful, or, to put it in other words, can have no obligations toward anybody. The persons who endow them with revenues, privileges, and benefices are but instruments in the hands of God for the greater good of his ministers. The duty of the clergy is, then, clearly to show themselves ungrateful for assumed benefits, were it only to fulfill the words of the prophet, who declares that you have only to give them meat if you wish them to declare war upon you.

INNOVATORS

Are all who, without first obtaining the consent of the theologians, take upon themselves to teach any doctrine which these distinguished men have never till then thought of. They (the theologians) alone have the right of revising, correcting, and explaining the eternal decrees of the Godhead, nay, even of manufacturing fashionable dogmas for the special use of the fair sex, who, as we all are well aware, are fond of change in all things, but especially in matters of religion.

INSPIRATION

A peculiar effect of divine flatulence emitted by the Holy Spirit, which hisses into the ears of a few men chosen of God, who uses them as a species of air-pipe to transmit his will to the vulgar, amazed at the marvels of his works.

INSTRUCTION (religious)

Consists in the relating of pious fables to, and combating the reason of, believers who are under instruction. These sublime functions belong exclusively to the clergy, who possess the divine right of rendering the peoples and nations under their yoke as crazy and as imbecile as the interests of the church require and the will of the priests chooses them to be.

INTERDICTION

A fearful chastisement now and again imposed by the heads of the Church on nations whose princes they want to bring to their senses. It consists in depriving communities of religious worship, ceremonies, and spiritual grace, without the aid of which the crops will not ripen nor the fruits of the earth give forth their abundance. In former days the popes were very successful in employing this remedy, but they are more sparing of it in these latter days, and this for the best of reasons.

INTEREST

Of all men living, the ministers of God are the most disinterested wherever their own interest alone is concerned; they never, under any circumstances, have any other interests in view than those of God and his spouse, the Church. Now, the domestic establishment of the pair being a rather expensive one, the priests are anxious that it shall be kept up on a suitable footing.

INTERPRETERS.

Pious pettifoggers, to whom the church hands over the arrangement of her affairs when they have become embarrassed. By their wonderful shuffling and chicanery, these pettifoggers would succeed in obtaining a verdict against common sense itself.

INVECTIVES

Polite and charitable expressions used by theologians among themselves or against their adversaries when they desire to conciliate things or surmount any difficulty that is opposed to them. Invectives are powerful arguments, but the stake and the pillory have proved themselves to be arguments more powerful still.

INQUISITION

A sacred tribunal composed of priests and monks independent of the civil power and possessing alone the right of judgment without appeal, both in their own cause and the cause of those who oppose them. With the aid of this holy tribunal the priests who authorize it are assured of reigning over the most orthodox, pious, and deluded subjects In the world, ever ready and willing to take up arms in the cause of the clergy against temporal power. It is to be regretted that the want of such a holy tribunal has not hitherto made itself felt in France.

JANSENISTS

Bastard Catholics who, in spite of the Holy Father, the clergy, and the court, persist in calling themselves orthodox. The grace that saves has not yet succeeded in getting presented at court, but in compensation she has on her side the *rue St. Honore,* the *Marais,* and the markets, without counting many lords of the parliament. The Jansenists are meek and honorable when they have not might on their side; but when might is with them, their charity sours in a greater or less degree. In spite of the austerity that characterizes them, their brows clear up from time to time at the contemplation of the notable miracles that God works in their favor. It is in Lent especially that their cheerfulness is remarkable. Not long since, Sister Francoise gave a private ball on a certain Good Friday in an alley in the *rue St. Denis*, and such was her cheerfulness on this occasion that she danced herself to death. (See Convulsionists.)

JERUSALEM

There are two towns of this name, the one situated in Judea and the other in the fiftieth degree of imaginary space. The latter is, according to St. John, in the Apocalypse, a beautiful city all built of diamonds and emeralds, rubies, and other precious stones. Christians who properly mortify themselves here below shall one day see it.

JESUITS

A company of very black and very warlike monks, who, some two centuries since, banded together to the end of reviving the faith, which was dying out of the earth. They are the janizaries of the pope, and not infrequently get his holiness into trouble. They are the depositaries of the penknife of the Church, the handle of which is at Rome. A short time since, Father Malagrida lost the blade in Portugal, and the brotherhood was dangerously wounded by it.

JESUS CHRIST

A name that once upon a time was taken by the Godhead when he went to make a short sojourn in Judea, where, failing to declare his right name and qualities, he was hanged as a spy. Had it not been for this lucky *quid pro quo* the human race had been lost and we should never have heard speak of the bull *Unigenitus*.

JEWS

A nation full of amenity and composed of lepers, misers, usurers, and scurvy rogues whom the God of the universe, delighted with their shining qualities, in former days fell in love with, an act which caused him to say and do a number of foolish things. This love has passed away, however, since the Jews hanged his son, and he will have no more to do with them except at such times as when the Inquisition roasts one of them and serves him up on his table as a special delicacy.

JUBILEE

A time of recreation and cheerfulness granted by the pope to his flock that they may sport and gamble in the spiritual meadows, which always contributes more or less to the manuring of the lands of the Church.

JUDEA

A holy and barren country which is about as vast as the Kingdom of Yvetot. This country, by an astounding miracle, produces to its kings as big revenues as the whole of Europe put together, the expenses of the tribe of Levi deducted.

JONAH

Was a scolding and wrathful prophet. He was three days in the belly of a whale, which, not being able to stand him any longer, vomited him forth, thereby showing what a hard morsel is a prophet to digest.

JUDGMENTS (rash)

Are forbidden by the Gospel, especially to laymen, who should never, under any circumstances, judge the conduct of the spiritual guides. If these should stumble upon a bishop or an abbe in any haunt of suspicious fame, they are bound to believe that the holy man is there for the salvation of souls and the greater glory of God, who cannot be angry with his creatures for enjoying themselves.

JUGGLERS

Quacks and mountebanks who, by their wonderful tricks of legerdemain, impose on the vulgar in all countries. The priests of false religions are knavish jugglers; the priests of the true religion are honest jugglers, and should be respected, particularly when we find ourselves within the reach of their magic wand.

JUSTICE (divine)

Has not the slightest resemblance in the world to human justice. In the meantime the theologians know that it is by an effect of theological justice that God visits on the whole human race the sin of one man; that it was through justice that he caused his beloved and innocent son to die to appease his own justice; that it is through justice that he condemns to eternal fire all those to whom he has refused his grace; that it is through justice that the priests condemn to the stake all who are not of their way of thinking. Hence it is that divine or theological justice has nothing in common with that which mankind calls justice.

JUST (the)

Are those of the Christians who enjoy the advantage of being agreeable in the eyes of God. The earth is theirs by right, and they may possess it if they are in number sufficient to do so.

KEYS (power of the)

Jesus Christ himself remitted the keys of heaven to his Church. They alone can open or shut the gates of paradise. The pope is the janitor; therefore, "no song, no supper."

KINGDOM OF GOD

The kingdom of God is not of this world; Christ himself has said it, but it is not one of his best sayings. If things were as they ought to be, the priests alone would command here below; but alas! the little faith to be found in princes often opposes them in their holy enterprises. Had mankind a sufficient dose of faith, it is kings and potentates who would be at the orders of the clergy.

KINGS

Are the chiefs or the heads of nations and the most humble servants of the priests, who, in a Christian country, should owe allegiance to none, and should command all. Kings are only made kings for the purpose of defending the clergy, supporting and enforcing their arguments, and, above all, of exterminating their enemies.

LAITY

Profane and unclean animals who have not the honor of feeding at the sacred rack. They are the beasts of burden of the priests, with this difference, that whereas it is generally the custom for the rider to feed the horse, in the Church of God it is, on the contrary, the horse that feeds him who bestrides him.

LAMB OF GOD

Jesus Christ. Scripture warns us to flee from the wrath of the lamb, who is, according to the Apocalypse, fiercer than a wolf and more irritable than a turkey-cock.

LATIN CHURCH

Is the church in which Latin is still chanted, though people have long since forgotten how to speak it. This is a very sensible and judicious custom, seeing that it suits the clergy that believers, like parrots, should not have the least idea of what they are uttering, and moreover should not be scandalized by the delectable things they find in their psalm books.

LAUGHTER

A Christian should be as grave as a donkey that is receiving a thrashing. Jesus Christ was never known to laugh, and indeed there is nothing to laugh at anyway, seeing that a Christian is in danger of falling, at any moment, into the boiling cauldron prepared for him by the divinity to the end of enjoying an eternal laugh at his expense. No, indeed; there is nothing to laugh at in the matter for any one concerned, except the priests, who laugh in their sleeve at the profits they derive from it.

LAW

A good Christian should never go to law; rather should he give up his coat and his pants, and everything that he hath. Churchmen never go to law; they are the most docile and easy creatures in the world on matters of business.

LAWS (canon)

A collection of the laws, ordinances, constitutions, decisions, bulls, etc., invented by the ministers of God to form the sacred jurisprudence that they have given to themselves. This special jurisprudence is against common sense, civil jurisprudence, the rights of kings, and even the rights of nature; all of which rights should and must yield to the right divine.

LEAGUE

A pious association formed in the sixteenth century by the Church of God, some of the salutary effects of which were the murder of a king of France, the plunging of the land into turmoil and dissensions, and the celebration of the holy ceremony of the mass by a heretic priest, who found himself none the worse for it.

LEGENDS

Wonderful and edifying stories which are now but seldom read, strong-minded and skeptical critics having thrown any number of wet blankets on the credulity of believers.

LENT

A time of mortification, fasting, and tears, by which some Christians more devout than others prepare themselves to eat of the paschal Lamb, whose flesh would be quite indigestible if persons did not fast and thoroughly purge themselves before partaking of it.

LETTERS

The Church stands in need of none such, seeing that her holy founders were ignorant and unlettered. The only letters that are useful to her are *lettres de cachet*.

LEVITES

The children of Levi, to whom, as a reward for their pious ferocity, the tender-hearted Moses offered the sacred functions of the priesthood. The tribe of Levi, at the command of Moses, had massacred the fellow-citizens of the latter, whom the high priest, Aaron, had caused to lie. Thus we see that our own priests of today, who have inherited the rights as well as all the zeal of the Levites, are quite justified in murdering any number of rogues who have been induced by priests into error.

LIBERTINES

This term should be applied to any man or woman who does not believe in religion. You cannot be at one and the same time a reasoning being and a moral one; only libertines and debauchees are capable of reasoning and doubting. Besides, it is a patent fact that not one single instance of libertinism or immorality has ever been found out against Christians.

LIBERTIES OF THE GALLICAN CHURCH

The French, who are a volatile people, frequently treat the pope in a very airy, off-hand way. Our magistrates are strong-minded men, who refuse to believe in his infallibility, who believe that he himself is but the servant of the Church, and who pretend that he has not received, like Samuel, the right of dethroning kings or even of poking his holy nose into their temporal affairs; all of which maxims must carry with them a strong smell of heresy, especially to a Roman nose.

LIBERTY OP THOUGHT

Should be repressed with the most rigorous severity. The priests think for the people, who have nothing else to think of than to pay generously those who spare them the trouble of thinking.

LIBERTY (political)

Is not much to the taste of the Church; despotism is far more profitable to her. When the prince is saddled, the whole nation is bridled, and forced to bend to the yoke of the Lord, which, as we all know, is and has been of the easiest.

LOGIC

According to the profane, is the art of reasoning; according to theologians, the art of non-reasoning one's self, or misguiding the reason of others. Theological logic becomes very convincing when it is backed by fire and sword.

LOVE (divine)

An accursed passion which corrupt nature inspires in one sex for the other. The God of the Christians is not gallant, and allows of no trifling on this head. Were it not for original sin, mankind would increase without love, and women would bring forth through the ear.

LOVE (self)

A fatal disposition of our corrupt nature which inspires in us a love for ourselves, a desire to preserve ourselves from all that is painful and disagreeable, and an ardent wish for our own personal welfare. Had Adam not fallen, we should, on the contrary, have hated ourselves, detested everything pleasant and agreeable, and have given no thought to our own preservation.

LUKEWARMNESS

Is a most reprehensible indifference shown by some Christians with regard to the most important subjects of salvation, and which may ultimately lead them to tolerance. The Christian temperament should be always at boiling heat. God vomits forth the lukewarm, and the heart of a woman turneth from a lukewarm lover.

LUST

A deadly sin, for which God will listen to no excuse or palliation. By a special effect of his grace, monks and priests are exempt from it. A rakish monk would be as bad as a reasoning being. In the meanwhile, fornication is permitted to priests, with, however, certain reservations.

LUXURY

The Church, like all women in general, has, in spite of all her spouse can say, a decided leaning toward dainty fare, and purple and fine linen. Her mother-in-law, the Blessed Virgin, would seem to share in this weakness and is never so gratified as when she is invested with a flaunting new gown.

MACERATION

An ingenious way of losing flesh. God loveth not big-bellied Christians, unless the monks of the order of St. Bernardine be the owners of such. Laymen must be very lean indeed before they may hope to slip through the gate of Paradise.

MAGIC

There are two sorts of magic — white or natural magic, and black magic, commonly known as witchcraft or the black art. The first is a holy art, and is daily practiced in the Church, the ministers of which are magicians, who oblige both God and the Devil to do whatever they ask them to do. Black magic is an unlawful practice as far as the laity is concerned, priests alone being allowed to have anything to do with the Devil.

MAHOMETANISM

A sanguinary religion whose odious founder willed that it should be established by sword and fire. The difference is palpable between such a religion and the religion founded by Christ, which teaches but gentleness and loving kindness, and whose sacred dogmas, in consequence, are established by the priests with fire and sword.

MAN

Man, in the ordinary sense, may be thus defined: An animal composed of flesh and bones, who walks on two legs, feels, thinks, and reasons. According to the Gospel and to St. James, man should neither feel, nor think, nor reason; nay, to make himself the more agreeable and acceptable, he should go about upon all fours, to the end that the ministers of the Lord might all the more easily get upon his back.

MAN (an honest)

It is materially impossible to be an honest man without a deep conviction that the Church is infallible, and that her priests are equally incapable of lying, or of deceiving themselves or others. It is clear that a man who does not fear damnation in the next world will never feel the necessity of honor in this one, and will sneer alike at the disdain and chastisement of the latter, as he scouts the idea of *punishment* in the former.

MANICHEISM

A heresy most justly condemned and detested by the Christians. The Manicheans admit in the universe two principles equal in power, which is abominable; the Christians admit an all-powerful

God whom the Devil may at any moment overthrow, which is most orthodox.

MARRIAGE

A state of imperfection of which, however, the Church has made sacrament. There is but one thing good about it, and that is, that it puts money in the way of the priests who have prudently invented hindrances to have the pleasure of selling dispensations to them.

MARTYRS

Devout and obstinate people, who put themselves in the way of being imprisoned, whipped, dismembered, and roasted, to the sole end of proving to the universe that their priests are not in the wrong. Every religion has its martyrs, but the true martyrs are those who have died for the true religion. The true religion is that which is not false, or that which the priests proclaim is the true one.

MARVELOUS (the)

The basis of all religions; any and everything that we do not understand; all and every thing that causes dotards and old women to open wide both eyes and ears. Those smart people who are wanting in faith can see nothing marvelous in the whole universe except it be the docility of mankind and the intrepid impudence of the priests, the marvels announced by the prophet Jeremiah, who says that priests never blush. *Facies Sacerdotum non erubuisant.*

MASS

In the Romish Church, is a succession of magical ceremonies, of prayers in good Latin, of juggling tricks, with a silver or golden goblet, that only a priest has the right to go through. The ceremony of Mass serves to remind God of the death of his beloved son, a circumstance that does as much honor to his tenderness as to his justice.

MATINS

Prayers chanted in the Romish Church in the middle of the night to prevent our Eternal Father, who is subject to snoring, from falling asleep over the needs and wants of his creatures.

MEDITATION

A pious Christian has nothing better to do in this world than to give himself up to the ceaseless meditation of the mysteries of his religion, a task that may amuse him for a very long time, especially if he tries to understand anything about them.

MELCHISEDEK

A priest who never had either father or mother. He was the figure or the model of the Christian priest who detaches himself from all the ties of blood to attach himself to the Church. A priest should forsake his father, and his mother, and his country when he enrolls himself beneath the sacred banner of the Church.

MENDICANTS

Friars who have vowed to God to possess nothing of their own, and to live at the expense of those who have something of their own. There cannot be too many of these in any state; the poor are the friends of God, and have at least for others a credit which they do not use for themselves.

MERCENARIES

Folks who do nothing. The priests of the Lord are not mercenaries; they frighten us for nothing, they quarrel among themselves for nothing, they persecute us for nothing, they trouble us and divide society for nothing, looking to God alone for the reward of their labors, provided, however, the community gees bail for him, or pays them in advance.

MERCY

The distinctive attribute of the God of the Christians, but assuredly not of his priests, who mercilessly burn and roast in this world and in the next whoever has not the advantage of being agreeable to them. Nevertheless, our bishops give proof of mercy in their mandamuses. It is by the help of divine mercy that they hold the bishoprics granted to them by kings at their most pressing solicitation.

MESSIAH

The liberator of the people of Israel. The latter had not the wit to recognize him as such beneath his assumed disguise of a working carpenter, who was not even so much as able to save himself from the gallows, but who in compensation saved all who believed in him from sin and death. It is needless to add that since Christ's expiation not one single Christian has been known either to sin or die.

METAPHYSICS

A most important and sublime science, by the help of which a man is enabled to arrive at a thorough knowledge of things of which his senses will not permit him to form an idea. All Christians are profound metaphysicians. Any pious prude will explain to you with imperturbable coolness what is the nature of a pure spirit, of an immaterial soul, and the grace that sufficeth to itself.

MILITANT

An epithet most fitting to the Church. So long as she is on the earth, so long must she cause men to wrestle with and fight against one another, to gain the guerdon thrown to them by the spectators, who are diverted by the strife; so long will she get up military executions for the extermination of those *not* diverted by the show, and who refuse to pay accordingly.

MIRACLES

Works that are supernatural, that is to say, contrary to the wise laws prescribed by the immutable Divinity to nature. With faith we can work as many miracles as we like; when faith declines, adieu to miracles, and nature is once more left to her own devices.

MISSIONARIES

A sacred order of recruiting sergeants, who, at the risk of being whipped, roasted, and devoured, go to the far-off lands to recruit souls in the cause of God, martyrs in the cause of the Church, and treasures for the prosperity of convents and monasteries. By the help of strong waters and the blaze of firearms, our missions have hitherto proved pretty generally successful.

MOLINISTS

People who, on the question of divine grace, have a system opposed to that of the Jansenists. The court, quite adept in questions of theology, has ever shown a sneaking kindness for the system of

Molina, which it has thoroughly examined. As for the clergy, it is usually on the side of those who hold the best of fat livings. The latter is never contradicted except by here and there a lousy fellow who is debarred from any share in the sacred pie.

MONEY

A source of crime from which the association of priests should endeavor to the utmost to relieve the faithful, to the end that these may walk with a lighter and less measured tread in the paths of salvation. Jesus Christ forbade his disciples to accept money, but the Church has since changed all that. In these our days, no money no priest; and, after all, this is but in obedience to the command contained in the book of Levites (xxvii 3, 18), "And the priest shall count his money."

MONKS (or Friars)

Are regularly ordained priests, that is to say, enrolled. They are clothed in white, grey, brown, and black, according to the uniform of their respective orders. Some wear their beard and some shave it off. These men are evidently useful to society, and have consequently the right of levying taxes thereon whenever and wherever they will. Monks and friars are the chief supporters of the Romish Church. Nations who have not yet entered upon the enjoyment of this useful commodity are affluent and wealthy, and consequently will be damned.

MOON

A place where, it is popularly believed, is to be found everything that is lost here below. If there be any truth in this, there is still hope that Christians may once more recover their wits and the fund they have given to their priest. In the meantime the moon has a notable influence over Christians, as likewise over the Church of Christ, which is rather crotchety and flighty.

MORALITY (Christian)

Is much more excellent than the worldly morality proper to philosophers, and which is the opposite. It consists of many prayers, much devotion, belief, zeal, gloom, malice, and idleness. Profane morality on the contrary, prescribes us to be just, laborious, indulgent, and benevolent. Hence we must conclude that the Christian religion gives no scope for morality here below.

MOSES

A prophet inspired of God who gave to him a holy and righteous law, which he was obliged to change later on, seeing that it had become worthless. Moses conversed familiarly with the back side of God. He was the meekest of men, as he himself tells us. Nevertheless he caused some thousands of the Israelites to be slaughtered, but he did this as a figure of the Church, who, though, as it is well known, the tenderest of mothers, now and again plays fierce and bloody tricks on her beloved children.

MORTIFICATIONS

Numerous ingenious inventions imagined by pious Christians to kill themselves slowly or render life insupportable. It is plain that the God of all goodness has endowed us with life and health only that we may have the honor and glory of slowly destroying both. We may not kill ourselves at one blow, for that would cut short the pleasure the Godhead takes in our sufferings, and prevent these sufferings from lasting long enough.

MUSTARD

A most precious commodity and very scarce in religion. Scripture tells us that a portion of faith not bigger than a grain of mustard-seed would suffice to move mountains. The Pope has for his part such a large quantity of mustard that a man is attached to his service to carry it for him; it is he who is designated as "The Mustard-Pot-in-Chief of the Pope."

MYSTERIES

Things we do not understand, but which we are bound to believe, nevertheless, which is very easy to do with the help of faith. God in his mercy, disgusted with the ignorance of mankind, came down to instruct them himself; he descended from his throne expressly to teach them that they should comprehend nothing of his teachings. Whenever you find in religious matters anything that puzzles the priests themselves to explain, anything in direct opposition to common sense, then content yourself that that is a mystery, a secret of the Church.

MYSTIC SENSE

Is a sense that no one can understand, or which renders the thing explained more obscure than it was before. Whenever a theologian meets with anything in the word of God quite the opposite of common sense, then he should seek for its mystic sense; and faith demands that you think he is right, though neither you nor he either understand the thing explained or the explanation that is given of it.

NATURE

Is the work of a God, wise, all-powerful, and perfect; nevertheless, nature has become corrupt. God has willed it so, doubtless to have an opportunity, now of diverting himself, now of getting mad. His bile is out of order, and if the management of his works were of too facile government, both he and the theologians would feel time hang heavy on their hands.

NEIGHBOR

A Christian should love his neighbor as himself. Now, a devout Christian is bound to hate himself and make his neighbor as wroth as possible, so as to gain the kingdom of heaven at his expense.

NOTHINGNESS

All opinions agree in this, that nothingness is that which we cannot affirm, or that which has none of the faculties we are able to judge of. "Such being the case, your Reverence, what is a spiritual being? What is a substance immaterial, or void of dimension, and color, and form? What is an angel? What is a devil? What is a —" "Stop, stop! my good man; these and such like are mysteries which it is given to neither you nor me to understand."

OBEDIENCE

It is better to obey God than man. Now, to obey God is to obey the clergy; whence it follows that a good Christian should obey his prince only in proportion as the wishes or demands of the prince beapproved by the clergy.

OBSCURITY

Portions of the Bible are sometimes obscure, and the same may be said of the holy religion revealed by God himself. Persons of weak faith are scandalized at this, but the devout bow down in silent adoration before any or everything that they cannot comprehend. A plain, simple, comprehensible religion would be but short lived; our holy interpreters would have nothing to tell us had the Godhead expressed himself clearly and plainly.

ODOR OF SANCTITY

The saints of the Lord are not, as a rule, sweet-smelling personages, but the odor exhaled from a capuchin friar, especially after his death, is more delightful to pious olfactories than the most exquisite perfumes to the noses of the godless.

OFFENSIVE

Any proposition that does not sound well in clerical ears merits this qualification. For instance, it is offensive to say that priests should not be paid in hard cash for the purely spiritual commodities they trade in.

OFFENSES

The all-powerful God, though in the enjoyment of an unchangeable felicity, nevertheless, to oblige his clergy, allows this felicity to be constantly troubled, and gets angry continually with the thoughts, words, and actions of his creatures. If God did not grow wroth from time to time, then good-bye to the clerical cash-box, and M. de St. Julian might as well shut up shop.

OFFERINGS

The God of the universe can need nothing; a pure spirit can eat but little, and that little, of necessity, of a purely spiritual nature. His priests, however, are not pure spirits, and he requires that they shall receive fat offerings; it is to this end solely that he showers his blessings over the face of the earth.

OMNISCIENCE

A quality exclusively suitable to God. Nevertheless, he affects to ignore what we are going to do, or that we are free in our actions. The Godhead communicates his omniscience to his priests. A theologian knows everything and cannot be taken at a disadvantage, especially with regard to things that are incomprehensible to any one else.

ORACLES

Answers of obscure and ambiguous meaning rendered in former times by the Devil, who is the Father of Lies, through the organs of pagan priests, a band of the most detestable rogues. These lying oracles have ceased since the advent of Jesus, from which period our oracles have invariably been rendered in the simplest, plainest, and most concise language.

ORATIONS (Funeral)

Discourses in the honor of the great ones of the earth, who are invariably, as we all know, very wonderful personages after their death. The makers of funeral orations cannot lie, seeing that they speak from the seat of all truth.

ORDER OF THE UNIVERSE

Is the marvelous arrangement and working of Nature as seen by those who look at her through the spectacles of Faith, which have the virtue of hiding from the eyes of those who wear them the disorders that exist in the universe. Through these glasses can be seen neither disease, nor crime, nor wars, nor earthquakes, nor intolerant theologians: all is in first-rate order when our sacrificers have well dined, and whosoever troubles their digestion is a disturber of public order.

ORDERS (Holy)

One of the most useful ornaments to the church, and which, without effort, increases and multiplies the tribe of Levi, so essential to the salvation of our souls. In the Romish and Anglican churches a bishop alone has the right of conferring this precious sacrament. By imposing his sacred paws on the skull of a profane one he causes to descend in a perpendicular line from heaven all the gifts of the Holy Ghost, especially the right of imposing on others.

ORDERS (Monastic)

Divers regiments of monks and friars who serve as volunteers in the army of God. They are in receipt of material pay from the community to protect them spiritually from the spiritual attacks of such spirits, and to bring down spiritual graces on their souls, which the bodies of the monks derive profit from likewise.

ORIGINAL SIN

A frolic which was enacted some seven thousand years ago, and caused a vast deal of commotion and disturbance both in heaven and earth. Every man, before he is born, takes part in this sin, through which men die and commit sin. The Son of God himself came down on earth to expiate this sin, but in spite of his efforts, and those of his Father, the stain still exists and will exist eternally.

ORTHODOX

Such are the opinions of those who are in the right, who are not heretics, and who have princes, and armies, and the hangman on their side. Orthodoxy, like the barometer, is apt to vary in Christian states, where it is always regulated by the sort of weather that prevails at court.

PAPISTS

A derisive epithet applied by Protestants to Catholics, the latter being docile Christians who give allegiance to the pope as vice-God here below, and who have not, like the former, sufficient strength of mind to submit their intellect only to a preacher of Geneva, or a Presbyterian minister, or a D.D. of Oxford. For the rest, no one will dispute the fact that a Christian of whatever denomination or sect he be, has the undoubted right to laugh at another Christian.

PABABLES

Apologues or indirect ways of expressing facts much affected by the Godhead in holy writ, doubtless for fear he should speak too plainly to the favored he wishes to instruct.

PARADISE

A place of delights, situated according to some in unknown austral regions, and, according to others, in the empyrean. The elect shall there, to all eternity, enjoy the pleasures of singing church music. Many persons have but a very slight desire to join these music parties, both through the fear of being ultimately bored by them and of finding themselves in very doubtful company.

PARROTS

Are considered by the Church as very useful animals, who, without understanding, nevertheless learn and faithfully repeat all that they are taught. (See Catechism, Christians, Education.)

PARTY-SPIRIT

In matters of religion this spirit essentially enables us to come to a wise judgment of things; it cannot be doubted that the side we have chosen to be on, or that our priests have chosen we shall be on, is the best of any.

PASSIONS

Movements essential to the preservation of man and inherent to his nature, since that nature became corrupt through original sin. Had it not been for That memorable *faux pas*, we should have been like stocks and stones, and consequently in the enjoyment of perfect felicity. A good Christian should have no other passions than those his priests inspire him with.

PASSION OF JESUS CHRIST

A lamentable tale of a God who was benevolent enough to let himself be whipped and crucified for the redemption of the human race. When on a certain day of the year (Good Friday) this story is told in all its details to the women and other devout persons of the community, they mourn, and groan and lament for having been so redeemed.

PASTORS

Those who have the charge of leading the flock of the Lord to graze. They have undertaken such charge through pure charity, only reserving to themselves the right of fleecing the flock and of sending to the slaughterhouse those among them whose fleece has not proved sufficiently abundant. Princes are the dogs of these shepherds of souls, and at their bidding bite with a sharpened tooth all sheep who stray or will not let themselves be shorn.

PATIENCE

A moral and Christian virtue which consists in supporting the ills we cannot or dare not avoid. God has specially charged the clergy to exercise the patience of princes, who are, as a rule, willful and hot-headed.

PATRONS

Are the household or tutelary gods of the Christians. They are specially interested in all who are named after them, St. John is the protector of all other Johns in the world, for instance. In like manner, animals, diseases, and calamities have their patrons, St. Rock having in his department the plague, St. Anthony the pigs, and St. Joseph the cuckolds and other horned cattle.

PEACE

The God of the Christians is called indifferently the God of peace and the God of armies. This contradiction is but apparent, however. God himself is a peaceable God, but his spouse is not by any means so peaceable as he. It is to keep her in a good temper that he sends his armies forth and sets Christians to fighting with each other. He must make war without to be able to maintain peace within. The Church is at rest only when she has everything her own way, or is able, without let or hindrance, to trouble the tranquillity of others.

PENITENCE

According to the Romish Church, is a sacrament which consists in accusing ourselves of the sins we have committed and showing a hearty sorrow for such commission. In all the religions of the world penitence is practiced; in other words, men voluntarily inflict suffering on themselves to gladden the heart of the Godhead.

PENTECOST

A solemn feast celebrated by the Church in commemoration of the descent of the Holy Spirit, under the figure of fiery tongues, on the heads of the Apostles, the Disciples, and certain holy females, who immediately began to wag them like so many bummers and magpies. As a consequence of this event, the successors of these holy men and women have undoubtedly acquired the right to prate to their hearts' content, and even to set the world on fire with their prating.

PEOPLE (the)

Are the pillars of the Church, her consolation in her afflictions, and the upholders of her power. The people are, as it is well known, profound theologians, and it is for them alone that the Church builds up her dogmas; those approved by the people cannot fail to be sound. The voice of the people is the voice of

God. In effect, God could hardly refuse the people anything they earnestly desired or anything that the priests earnestly desire they should earnestly desire.

PERSECUTIONS

Sure and loving means employed by the Church to bring back to her bosom those who have strayed, and render herself more lovely in their eyes. The Church herself has frequently suffered persecution, but always wrongfully so; while the persecutions she inflicts on others are ever lawful and holy. To have the right to persecute, one should be in the right one's self, and it suffices to be in the right not to be in the wrong. The Church is never in the wrong, but above all is she not so when she has force on her side to prove that she is in the right.

PETER

A poor fisherman, and not over-smart. He made a handsome fortune, however, and became prince of the Apostles, owing to the fact that his name gave his Lord an opportunity to unbend his mind by making a pun on it, which pun ultimately furnished the foundation for the kitchen of our Holy Father the Pope.

PHILOSOPHERS

Are the avowed friends of wisdom and of common sense, or, in other words, knaves, thieves, jail-birds, blasphemers, detestable in the eyes of the Church, and deserving of nothing from society at large but the pillory and the stake. These rascals have the impudence to warn the people that while looking up to heaven, as they are told to do, the strings of their purses are being cut here below.

PHYSICAL PREMONITION

Is a warning impulse by which, according to M. Boursier, God disposes man, before he acts, to act in a way at once in conformity with his will and the free will of man, which the Godhead is not allowed to touch, doubtless for fear that man should have the merit of acting with wisdom purely through the agency of free will.

PHYSICIANS

The priests are the physicians of souls. They give us the itch that we may have the pleasure of scratching ourselves. With regard to the medicines they use, they most frequently prescribe purgatives, cupping, and blisters. The pills they give us are very bitter and are rarely well gilded except for themselves.

PILGRIMAGE

A pious practice much in favor in devout communities, and consists principally in tramping the country to pay a visit and a bottle or two to some far-off saint or his nearest friends, which politeness is reciprocated by said saint by granting to the pilgrim the grace of getting drunk, if a man, and of giving birth to a little Christian nine months after said visit, if a woman.

PLATO

An Athenian philosopher and one of the fathers of the Christian Church, which should, without further mention, have placed him in her calendar. It is to him she owes a great many of her dogmas and articles of faith, without counting a goodly-number of mysteries.

POLITICS

The Christian Church is the chief support and upholder of politics; it is she who maintains the tranquillity of states, obedience to the laws, etc., etc. She enjoins obedience to the governors provided the governors show themselves submissive to her authority; in a word, her priests are a body in the state, whose interests are invariably the interests of the state provided the state itself takes into account the interests of the priests.

POMPS OF SATAN

Every Christian renounces these on receiving the sacrament of Baptism. It often happens, however, that he forgets his engagements on this head; the priests are the only Christians that never lose sight of them.

PONTIFFS

This word is derived from "pontifex;" a maker of bridges. Our pontiffs are spiritual architects who construct a spiritual bridge by the aid of which Christians cross over into paradise — far above the sloughs of reason and common sense.

POOR IN SPIRIT (the)

In the language of the profane, the poor in spirit are imbeciles and idiots; in the language of the Christians, they are ultra-smart persons, who, in this world, simulate imbecility the more effectually to astonish the cherubim and seraphim in paradise with their brilliant sallies and witty *mots*. This is why the Church shows a marked preference for the foolish among her children and holds but of little or no account the smart ones.

POPE

Usually an old priest chosen by the Holy Spirit to be the vicar of his brother here below. This accounts for the high intellectual capacity that has ever distinguished our popes, who have never been known to rave, or mouth, or talk gibberish, in spite of what the Jansenists, and those other fellows, the Protestants — who really in this instance carry too far freedom of thought — may think to the contrary.

POPULATION

Is injurious to Christian states, where, if things were as they ought to be, every one should hold to celibacy. Many are called and few are chosen. The more numerous the population of a country, the greater the number of reprobates it contains. Therefore is it that population is always injurious to a state.

POVERTY

In the Christian religion there is nothing but poverty to be seen on any side. Christ was poor, and was even a poor God; the Apostles were poor devils; the bishops are poor saints; monks make vows of poverty; priests make trade in very poor commodities, which are purchased by poor people, who pay a high price for them. The possessions of the clergy belong to the poor, whence it follows that it is most fitting and proper to despoil the poor to enrich the priests.

QUACKS

The sincere friends of the human race, whose sole end and aim in life is the benefit and well-being of its members. There are two classes of quacks — the sacred and the profane. The latter are arrant rogues, one and all; the former are honest and virtuous men who sell by permission of the king and his chief physician the spiritual antidotes. Their usual way of proceeding to cure is to make us first of all very sick, that we may the better appreciate the efficacy of their nostrums.

QUAKERS

Are the followers of an abominable sect which offers a most dangerous example in this, that it has hitherto continued to do without priests, a thing that is contrary to the interests of the Lord. Hence it will be seen that Quakers are not such cowards as those that are not Quakers.

QUARRELS (theological)

Important disputes, which, to the greater glory of God and the diversion of his spouse, now and again arise between the infallible organs of the divine will. Infallibility existing on both sides, agreement between the disputants is not always easily obtained. These quarrels are useful to the Church, inasmuch as when people dispute on the form of a thing they usually let the thing itself alone.

It is of the utmost importance that princes and potentates take part in theological disputes, each action on their part giving much greater weight to such disputes, and, which is more important still, preventing them from ending too promptly.

QUESTIONS (theological)

These are of the very highest importance. It is, for instance, an important question to know whether or not Adam had a navel; whether the apple he ate was a green or a ripe one; whether it is necessary to believe that Toby's dog wagged his tail; whether the Bull Unigenitus is an article of faith; if the Son of God could have come to us under the form of a milch cow, etc., etc. We may likewise class under the head of theological questions the tortures inflicted by the Holy Inquisition on heretics to make them confess to crimes they never dreamed of.

RABBI

A Hebrew word signifying master. Jesus Christ forbade his disciples to allow themselves to be called "master;" hence it is, doubtless, that his successors revel in such titles as "your reverence," "your lordship," "your eminence," "your holiness," etc.

RACA (a fool)

It is forbidden in the Gospel to call one's brother Raca; nevertheless, the clergy advise us so to call him if he be not of our opinion, if we have an opinion, or of the opinion of the clergy, if we have none of our own.

REASON

Is of all things in the world the most hurtful to a reasoning being. God only allows it to remain with those whom he intends to damn, and in his goodness takes it away from those he intends to save or render useful to the Church. If reason had any part in religion, what then would become of faith? However, it is well to listen to reason, whenever by chance her promptings agree with clerical interests.

REDEMPTION

A Christian is bound to believe that the God of the universe by consenting to die has redeemed mankind from the slavery of sin. Nevertheless, mankind goes on sinning all the same, which proves that the mystery of the redemption is of notable use to mankind.

REFORM

Since the foundation of Christianity, which is, as we all know, the masterpiece of the divine wisdom, the priests have been unceasingly occupied in reforming it. The devil is ever trying to derange the divine machine of salvation, and up to this it would seem that the Holy Ghost has never yet been able to thoroughly repair the damages he inflicts on it.

REFUGEES

Heretics whom France wisely and prudently rid herself of, and forced into exile. She has not injured herself in the least by so doing; pure faith remains with her, and that faith will suffice to guard her from all attempts of heretical nations against her. God, who is orthodox, will assuredly give her triumph over them.

REFUSAL OF THE SACRAMENTS

Like the dog of Jean de Nivelle, the priests don't always go where they wanted to go. Towards the forty-eighth degree of north latitude they frequently refuse absolutely to administer the sacraments to those who ardently desire to partake of them when dying, but in compensation they endeavor to force those spiritual messes fairly down the throats of of others who haven't the least appetite for them, a manner of acting doubtless dictated by the profound wisdom that invariably characterizes the pastors of the Churoh.

REGICIDE

A species of maternal chastisement administered by the Church herself to princes and potentates who may not happen to show her priests all the respect that is due to them. The profane cry out against regicides commanded by the Church, probably because those ignorant persons do not know that in ancient Rome parents enjoyed the right of putting their children to death.

RELICS

Pious and devout Catholics are imbued with a deep veneration for certain sacred carrion, which, as we all know, possesses the power of operating very great miracles in favor of those who believe. The breeches of St. Paris have cured more diseases than the whole of the faculty of Paris.

RELIGION

A system of doctrine and of conduct invented by God himself for the good of the priests and the salvation of our souls. There are many religions on the earth, but the only true religion is that of our forefathers, who were much too wise to allow themselves to be deceived. All other religions are but absurd superstitions, and should be abolished if possible. The true religion is the one we are accustomed to, or to which it might be dangerous to show any opposition. The religion of our princes, in particular, is marked with the indelible characters of truth.

REPARATION

We are bound to repair the injury we have done our neighbor, and the simplest and shortest way of doing this is to hand over to the priests the money we have stolen from our fellow-citizens. Reparation is assured when the Church is satisfied.

REPENTANCE

To obtain the remission of his sins a Christian should feel a hearty sorrow for actions he possibly took great pleasure in committing. An act of contrition suffices to make one's peace with God, which is very convenient for Christians who, in spite of their contrition, have no intention of mending their ways.

REPROBATES

All those whom the God of all goodness has destined to divert him eternally by their contortions, cries, and groans from out the fires which he has prepared for them. God is a just God, and owes nothing to any one, and consequently does too much honor to reprobates even by diverting himself at their expense, thereby showing that he is their master, a fact which otherwise they might be tempted to doubt.

RESIDENCE

The pastors of the Church are held to reside in the midst of their respective folds, to lead them to green pastures. There are, however, certain bishops who prefer to dwell in courts. The flock needs nothing when the shepherd is well fed.

RESPONSE

To respond in theology means to reply in the most abusive terms, to yell, to invoke the aid of the secular arm against all who dispute the opinions of the clergy. These responses are not altogether satisfactory, neither do they fully suffice to solve the difficulties in contention; but those who have faith will find them unanswerable, and the unbelieving may think what they like on the matter.

RESURRECTION

Jesus Christ rose again from the dead. We are assured of this by a number of very credible apostles and a few holy women, who could not have been deceived, without counting Jerusalem, which saw nothing of the circumstance. Christians believe firmly that they in their turn will rise again, or in other words, that their spiritual souls will once more regain their material bodies, and each one enter into possession once more of every atom of flesh and bone that belongs to him.

RETREAT

It is salutary for pious Christians to live retired, and separated from the world; this is calculated to make them sour, unsociable, and, above all, to heat and excite their brain. The society of men spoils us, and is a stumbling-block in the way of our salvation by preventing us from giving ourselves wholly and entirely to the contemplation of the sacred truths we shall never be able to understand.

REVELATIONS

Manifestations of the divine will made by the Almighty in person to certain of his chosen creatures. The word revelation is derived from *rever* (to dream, to have visions). The Godhead has revealed himself to every country on the earth, but the only true revelation is that of the dreamers who have dreamed for us. The safest thing is to believe so, anyway, priests having in abhorrence any truth that is not their truth.

REVOLTS

A spirit of pious bickering and opposition sometimes shown by the clergy towards princes and rulers of nations. A Christian may lawfully rebel against his sovereign when the pope counsels such action on his part, or when it is profitable to the clergy; in such cases it is the sovereign who has rebelled against the pope, or against the clergy, in other words, against God himself.

RICHES

Are an insurmountable obstacle to salvation. Rich men are as a rule too fat and portly to glide with ease into the narrow path which leadeth to righteousness. Should a rich man desire to enter on that path he must fast beforehand for many days, or get his fat melted down by the priests, who in a very short space of time will make him slim enough to obtain the object of his desire.

RITES

Pious usages and venerable formulas observed by our venerated professors of legerdemain, and to be found in sacred scrolls called rituals. Unbelievers scoff at all the rites, practices, and ceremonies of the Church, but she clings to such, and with reason, seeing that they bring grist to the clerical mill, which, were it to cease grinding, then religion must die of starvation.

ROMANS

A people renowned in other times, who, by right of conquest, made themselves masters of the whole world, and to the right of whom has succeeded the right divine of a priest, who, by dint of arguments, has conquered Europe. Those of the Christians who have submitted to this priest call themselves Roman Catholics; his legions are composed of Capuchin friars, gray friars, Franciscan friars, white friars, the Jesuits forming the praetorian cohorts, the bishops being his military tribunes, and the kings of Europe his purveyors and caterers as long as their faith holds out.

SACERDOTAL

A generic title designating an order of men, who, having sanctified themselves, spread themselves over the face of the earth. Their functions are to annihilate human reason, to invent wonderful tales and fables to quarrel with and persecute all who do not believe them, and to ask and exact from those who do a very high price for their important services. The religions of this world are numerous and various, but the priesthood is the same in all places, a fact which doubtless goes to prove that it is of origin divine.

SACRAMENTS

Are sacred signs and ceremonies by the help of which the ministers of the Lord call down from heaven a whole cargo of spiritual graces for believers, and cause the purses of the laity to pass by magic from their profane breeches pockets into the sacred ones of the clergy. According to some Christians, there are seven sacraments, but others won't have so many. These latter are evidently in the wrong, for we cannot have too much of a good thing.

SACRED

That which is not profane. As a general rule, everything that it suits the priests to impose on the credulity of the laity is sacred. The persons of priests, their possessions, their rights, their discussions, all these are evidently sacred things, and damned be he who dares to touch them.

SACRIFICES

In former days, the Most High kept a very sumptuous table; men, children, oxen, sheep, and the firstlings of the flocks were served up to him. Nowadays things have changed; his spouse has put him on diet, and the only dish she allows to he served on his table is his own son, and even him the priests themselves devour. The celestial pantry would be but in a sorry condition were it not for the roasts provided by the Holy Inquisition and for the princes of the earth making war on each other whenever the clergy hint that God is very wroth on an empty stomach.

SACRILEGE

A dreadful word invented by the priests to designate a fearful crime which is committed by any one touching with a profane hand anything they, the priests, have proclaimed sacred. Anything that wrongs the priests wrongs God, who is a severe God, Hence it is evident that to take from God, who is the sovereign owner of heaven and earth, is a far more heinous crime than to take from the poor, who have nothing. The richer the despoiled, the greater the crime of the despoiler; thus, he who robs the Lord shall be burnt, he who robs a rich man shall be hanged; but he who robs the poor shall have nothing to fear.

SAINTS

Are heroes of a certain type, and very useful to peoples and nations, who, by dint of praying, fasting, flagellations, etc., have immortalized themselves in the memory of believers, and have been ranked, like so many onions, in the calender, principally for having been all their lives useless to others and a torment to themselves.

SANCTUARY (right of)

In many truly Christian states the churches and monasteries thereof enjoy the right of affording a safe retreat to murderers, rogues, and thieves, to shield them from the rigors of the law; a custom very profitable to society at large, and which must render the ministers of the Church very dear to the heart of every ruffian.

SAMUEL

A very ill-tempered prophet and Jew who had but a very superficial knowledge of the rights of individuals and communities. He made mincemeat of other nations than his own, made and unmade kings, his own into the bargain, but for all this was rather good-natured than otherwise when he had his own way.

SATISFACTION

Christ in dying satisfied his father for the sins of mankind. By his death men were redeemed from sin and yet God the father still claims the debt. Therefore we must infer that the divine justice requires to be paid again the debts for which she has already given a receipt.

SCANDAL

Is any action which may become to others a source of sin and transgression. The ministers of the Lord never give cause for scandal, and nothing would be more scandalous than to say they scandalize us. Only unbelievers are scandalized by the conduct of scandalous priests. When believers see a scandalous priest, they should pluck out their eyes, in accordance with the words of scripture.

SCHISMATICS

Relatively to Roman Catholics, are Christians who refuse to acknowledge the pope as the head of the Church, but in reality are but a pack of idiots who cannot see that by thus acting they expose themselves to have the gates of Paradise slammed in their faces by St. Peter, who, now the janitor of heaven, was nevertheless once a pope himself.

SCHOOL

The arena whence our holy gladiators issue forth to come and do battle for and fight over the evident truths revealed by God himself. It is on the masses that the most powerful blows aimed by these doughty champions at each other most generally fall, which is in itself a most delectable miracle.

SLOTH

Is a very deadly sin, which consists in neglecting the pious practices to the exercise of which the priests attach the salvation of souls. A layman should be active and diligent, to the end of paying the priests for their services, and should be ready to fight their battles if necessary. As for the priests, they should do nothing but pray, sing, and quarrel among themselves when they have the capacity to do so.

SOLOMON

Was the wisest of kings. God himself endowed him with the gift of wisdom. He was accordingly a much greater rake than his papa, which is saying a great deal. From the midst of his five hundred wives this saint proclaimed that all is vanity.

SON OF GOD

Is the same thing as the son of man. The son of man is the same thing as the son of God; his father and God his father is the same thing as his son and as the Holy Ghost. This language may seem rather confused to persons of slight faith, but pious people will readily understand it.

SORBONNE

A royal manufactory of doctors of the Church with whom France is annually benefited. These doctors leave her sheltering arms armed *cap-a-pie* for the fight, and only require about half a score of years to learn all things necessary for the salvation of the souls of the peoples they are to indoctrinate.

SORCERIES

The Holy Ghost, as we may see in the Bible, formerly believed in such; likewise our forefathers for many centuries; but in these, our days, we accord but slight credence to them, and, in fact, shall very soon discard belief in anything.

SPIRIT

Every one knows what a spirit is. It is that which is not matter. Whenever you are at a loss to comprehend how a cause acts, you have but to tell yourself that such cause is a spirit, and then you will be fully enlightened.

STERCORANISTS

Certain persons who entertain the absurd opinion that the consecrated bread of the Eucharist— that is to say, changed into God — is rendered to the stool like any other aliment. Theologians were for a long time divided as to the ultimate destination of the God contained in the Eucharist after his reception into mortal stomachs, but have ultimately agreed that God alone knows what becomes of the Eucharist after we have received it.

STUDY

To a profound theologian consists in puzzling his brains and filling his pate with words to which neither himself nor any one else not endowed with the utmost degree of divine penetration can attach the slightest reasonable sense. With regard to the laity, study consists in learning Latin and the submission due to the priesthood.

SUICIDE

It is forbidden a Christian to end his days suddenly or to kill himself at one blow, but he may kill himself bit by bit, little by little, and then have nothing to fear. Indeed, such conduct on his part will be looked upon by other Christians as so edifying, so meritorious, that he may even hope to die in the odor of sanctity and even have his name in the almanac if he can manage to work a few miracles.

SUPERSTITION

Any practice or form of religion to which we are not accustomed. Any worship that is not offered up to the true God is false and superstitious. The only true God is the God of our priests; the only true worship is that which seems the most fitting to them, and to which they have accustomed us from our earliest childhood; and other worship is clearly superstitious, false, and even ridiculous.

SWEETNESS (Evangelical)

Consists in inculcating faith by dint of abuse, threats, and tortures. It is by the aid of such "sweetmeats" as these that the Church causes her children to swallow the pill of faith.

SWORD

Jesus Christ, for the greater good of the human race, came with the sword; the Church, who is subject to losing her temper now and again, has two swords in her arsenal, the spiritual sword and the temporal sword, the first of which kills the soul, the last the body. With these she brings people to their senses. Besides these two swords, she has in her possession a very small cutlass, but this she hides with care, for fear it should be taken from her, and only uses it on great and important emergencies. (See regicide.)

TE DEUM

A hymn of jubilation that is sung in Christian churches every time that a Christian prince has enjoyed the advantage of slaughtering hosts of his fellow-Christians and of causing to be slaughtered hosts of his Christian subjects.

TEMPTATION

The Most High once in a while subjects men to temptation to enjoy the pleasure of punishing them afterwards if they are idiots enough to fall into the snare. However, he usually gets the devil to tempt them, who has no other *earthly* function than to scoff at him and pervert and debauch his servants. Hence we see that the Most High, in his inscrutable decrees, diverts himself by playing tricks on himself.

TEMPORAL

That which is not eternal. Temporal power, existing for but a time, should be subordinated to spiritual power, which has no end. In the hands of the latter the former becomes likewise spiritual, eternal, and divine, and if the ministers of the church show such ardent zeal in its defense it is because they have given themselves to God, who is a pure spirit, but who, nevertheless, has an eye to the temporal blessings of this world, without which his spiritual ministers could not subsist.

TESTAMENT

The immutable God has made two in his life, the one called the Old and the other the New Testament. The Church holds to the former, but in so far as her hereditary interests are concerned, has adopted the latter in its entirety, its language being so precise and unequivocal that no possible dispute can arise among those who are called to the inheritance it promises. In the dark ages, that is to say, when the faith was lively and held its own, the testaments of laymen were declared null and void unless they bequeathed to the Church such a portion of their worldly goods as to fully satisfy her.

TESTIMONY

In the ordinary affairs of life, a person bearing testimony or acting as a witness is expected to be enlightened, sensible, and disinterested. In religion, those on the word of whom we are required to believe incredible things are pious ignoramuses, fanatical prophets and martyrs, priests who live on the fat of the land by bearing testimony to the fine things that we wot not of and yet we believe them.

THEOCRACY

A beautiful form of government, invented by Moses for the convenience of the tribe of Levi, and in which God alone is the sovereign, and consequently his beloved priests are the masters of the bodies and souls of men. This divine government should subsist in all places, but especially in Christian lands, whose princes should be but the valets of the clergy.

THEOLOGY

A science profound, supernatural, and divine, which teaches us to reason on that which we don't understand and to get our ideas mixed up on that which we do. Thus it is evident that theology if the noblest and most valuable science there is, all the others confining themselves to known and consequently despicable objects. Without theology empires could not subsist, the church would perish, and the nations would not know what to think about wars, gratuitous predestination, and the bull Unigenitus, concerning which last it is of vital importance that people have the most precise conception.

THESIS

In theology the term thesis is applied to grave, solemn disputations in public, in the course of which young theologians are in the habit of bruising each other's heads to the sole end of demonstrating the saving efficacy of their salve, or, in other words, of faith. With the Christians the thesis has taken the place of the Olympian games with the Greeks, the Exercises with the Romans, and the Conferences with the philosophers, who were but pagans and ignoramuses in matters of theology.

THOUGHTS

God is grievously offended by the voluntary movements of the brain of man, and especially so if those movements are not directed by the clergy. The Almighty will assuredly damn all who do not think with the priests, who possess the exclusive right of thinking for others. Hence it is that the clergy are so particular about the consciences of believers for fear that objectionable ideas should somehow or other get smuggled into their heads.

TIARA

The tiara is a triple crown, which, for the plenitude of his power in heaven, on earth, and in purgatory, his holiness the pope has a right to wear.

TIME

Time, which is so precious in the estimation of the profane, is of no account in the eyes of the Church. Her holy ministers lay it on us as a duty to lose as much time as possible in pious practices and pastimes. In effect, what is time compared to eternity?

TOLERANCE

A most impious system, and contrary to the views of the clergy. It can only be practiced by those Christians whose lack of zeal leads them to betray the interests of the Church, by allowing every one to think in his own way on certain questions; and especially on such questions as no one can understand. The Church knows her own interests better than any one else, and has never countenanced tolerance. Sects have ever detested each other, persecuted each other, and exterminated each other; and we have reason to hope they will go on in this way till the end of the world, if the Christian religion holds out till then.

TONSURE

A sacred operation performed on the hair of a layman who is desirous of enrolling himself in the ranks of the clergy, or in other words, who is desirous of living at the expense of others. This preliminary ceremony is intended to teach him who has been tonsured that his principal functions thenceforward will be to fleece his fellow-citizens, if the grace of God provides him with a good pair of scissors.

TRADITION

Tradition, in theology, is the word of God, received by pious, enlightened men, and handed down and transmitted to the Christians of the present time intact, and without any alteration whatever. As we see, tradition has been miraculously preserved. As a rule, men add to or detract from the things they hear and see, but such was not the case with the apostles, and our priests are too honest to alter or impair it.

TRANSUBSTANTIATION

According to the doctrines of the Christians, the God of the universe is obliging enough to change himself into a morsel of bread whenever a priest requests him to do so.

ULTRAMONTANES

Are all who live beyond the mountains. The Jansenists pretend that it would be a delectable thing if they would be sent over the bridges, a "consummation devoutly to be wished" for by the Italians.

TRINITY

An ineffable mystery adopted by Christians, who received it from the divine Plato; it is a fundamental article of our holy religion. With the help of this mystery, one God makes three Gods and three Gods make but one. The dogma of the Trinity can alone seem absurd to people who do not understand Plato. This father of the Church conceived three manners of considering the Divinity; of his power our holy doctors have made a Father with a venerable beard; of his reason they have made a son, emanating from this father, and hanged to stay his wrath and vengeance; of his goodness they have made a Holy Ghost, transformed into a pigeon; such is this mystery, and nothing more.

UNIVERSITIES

Are very useful establishments for the clergy, and are wisely confided to the care of its members, who zealously endeavor to raise up and fashion within their precincts any number of pious citizens, very devout, very zealous, very poor in spirits, very useless to society at large, but very helpful and useful to the clergy.

UNIGENITUS

A word with which begins a most interesting bull from the pope, and which for upwards of fifty years has kept France on the broad grin, without counting other results, such as an enormous increase in the paper trade, the distribution of two hundred thousand *lettres-de-cachet,* the rendering of a million mandamuses, and the writing of some very fine essays for the edification of the fish-women, and to give fuller exercise to the pious cackling of the court devotees.

UNITY

Every Christian should firmly believe that there is but one God. Were it not for divine revelation we should never have thought of this. In the mean time, every Christian is bound to worship three Gods who unjustly enjoy the sovereign divinity. Thus, according to the algebraic equations of our theologians, one is equal to three and three are equal to one. He who fails to perceive the exactitude of this arithmetic is of a surety wanting in faith and deserves to be damned.

UNITY OF THE CHURCH

As God is one, the Church is one. We cannot doubt of this when we consider the entire unity of dogmas, sentiments, and opinions that has ever existed in the midst of Christians from the very foundation of the Christian religion. This unity assuredly bears the impress of the finger of God.

USURY

God has promised the Jews that they should enjoy the practice of usury as well as that of thieving, but the Christians; that is to say, Christian laymen, are forbidden both, their clergy alone having the right to trade in usury, and even to draw big dividends from shares they never paid for.

USURPATION (Ecclesiastical)

There are persons wanting in faith who assert that the Church has more than once exercised rights that are not hers; had they faith, they would understand that the Church *cannot* usury, seeing that she exercises the rights of her spouse, whose rights are unlimited. The true usurper is he who hinders the Church from usurping those powers and rights which the laity is incapable of using without abusing.

VANITY

Outside of theology all is vanity in this world, and it is only in the next that we shall enjoy anything stable or solid. There it will be given us to judge of the solidity of the edifices raised up by our priests, though even here below their culinary department seems to be built on a pretty solid foundation.

VAMPIRE (The)

Is a dead body which sucks the blood of a living one. Strong-minded people may perhaps scoff at the idea of such a marvel, but they have only to open their eyes and they will assuredly behold the sight of a dead body sucking the blood of the living body of the human society. (See monks, priests, clergy.)

VASES

All men are vases, even as St. Paul saith. Some are of fine porcelain, of the ornamental kind, which God delighteth to place on the mantels and other parts of his dwelling to adorn and beautify it, while others are vases of the vilest potter's earth, which he is everlastingly scrubbing and scouring after having himself soiled them.

VENGEANCE

The God of the universe, according to the Bible, is vindictive, revengeful; therefore his ministers are bound to imitate him and enter into his views. The God of vengeance would be very wroth if his ministers failed to avenge him, and he is always avenged when his priests are.

VIATICUM

When a Catholic Christian is about to take a long journey, the church, like the good mother she is, gets him ready for the road, and, for fear his soul should faint by the way, garnishes his stomach with a wafer, a light and wholesome species of nourishment and quite sufficient for a soul on its travels.

VIRTUES (Moral)

Are only useful to human society, but are of no use whatever to the clergy. Thus they are but negative virtues, but may have some good in them if joined to evangelical virtues or to those called theological virtues.

VIRGIN (The)

Is the mother of the Son of God and the mother-in-law of the Church. She was spiritually overshadowed by God the Father, who, being but a pure spirit, did not, of course, consummate the marriage.

VISION

A species of magic lantern which the eternal Father has from the beginning been in the habit of exhibiting to his saints, his prophets, and his favorites of one and the other sex. Women, madmen, and rogues are the persons whom the Divinity in preference favors in this wise.

VISION (Beatific)

All those who in this life carefully shut their eyes at the eminent risk of their noses and shins and other portions of their corporal being, shall, in the life to come, enjoy such clear and piercing vision as to contemplate, face to face and without winking, the splendors of the Spirit that fills the universe.

VISIBILITY

Is a character of the true church, which should be visible, and which sometimes renders her palpable, especially when she gets on the high horse; then all other churches hide themselves and become invisible.

VOCATION

An inward and irrepressible voice of the divinity which calls on a boy or a girl of fifteen years to imprison himself or herself in a convent and to renounce all that is pleasant and agreeable for the remainder of his or her life. A vocation for the ecclesiastical state is a holy desire for benefices inspired by God himself in the hearts of younger sons and others who find themselves impelled by an unconquerable inclination to be utterly useless in the world and to their fellow-men.

VULGATE

The Latin version of the holy scriptures, inspired by the Holy Spirit, who doubtless was better acquainted with the Hebrew tongue than he was with the Latin one, for a perusal of the Vulgate will convince any one that the Most High does not speak quite such good Latin as that reprobate Cicero.

VIRTUES (Theological)

That is, necessary to theologians, or which have for object the utility of the clergy. They are Faith, Hope, and Charity. If these virtues, in themselves, are not of much utility to society at large, they are most useful to the priesthood. Faith delivers over to them those who are led on by hope, and the charity of these clothes the priests in comfortable raiment and gives them the wherewithal to fare sumptuously every day.

VOWS (Monastic)

Promises solemnly made to God to be useless to ourselves and to everybody else; to pass our lives in pious poverty, in holy itching and scratching, in holy submission to the will of a holy monk or a holy termagant, who to divert himself or herself makes life a hardship to those who are idiots enough to submit themselves to their yoke.

WARS OF RELIGION

Copious and salutary blood-lettings prescribed by the physicians of souls for the bodies of those nations whom God in his goodness desires to endow with a pure doctrine. They have been of frequent practice since the foundation of the Christian faith, and have indeed become necessary, for otherwise Christians might burst with the plenitude of the grace that is lavished on them from above.

WICKED

God is infinitely good, but it has been found expedient to make him more wicked and vicious than the devil himself. With a too lenient God the priests would do but a sorry trade.

WILL (Free)

Man is free, otherwise his priests could not damn him. Free will is a gift with which by special favor God has endowed the human race, and by the help of which we enjoy above all other animals the faculty of being damned to all eternity if our free will be not in accord with the will of the Almighty, the latter in this way being enabled to enjoy the pleasure of punishing him whose will he has left free to thwart and anger him.

WIND

A very precious commodity sold by our sacred conjurors at a very high price to us Christians, to aid us to a sail in St. Peter's bark. The special winds dealt in by the clergy are apt to produce tempests and storms, according to the words of Holy Writ, "Thou shalt sow the wind and reap the whirlwind."

WOMEN

Christianity, as a rule, shows but scant courtesy to pretty women. The old and ill-favored alone of the sex would seem to find favor in the eyes of the Lord and of his ministers.

WORD OF GOD

An infallible oracle in which in every religion the priests of the Most High trade in his name; the God-head, for the rest, is good-natured enough to never give them the lie. "Silence gives consent," says the popular axiom, and accordingly it would seem that God invariably consents to the word of the priests. The word of the Lord, say the Christians, is a two-edged sword, or, in other words, a butcher's knife, which, in whatever way you handle it is sure to injure you.

WORD (The)

Is the Logos of Plato, the divine wisdom, the eternal reason, of which our theologians have made a God, or, if you will, a man. We therefore firmly believe that the reason of the Godhead was made man to enlighten mankind, and, above all, to teach them that the divine reason did not intend that they should enjoy reason *en masse*, but only those of their number who were priests.

WORKS (Pious)

This term is applied in general to all endowments, legacies, presents, foundations, etc., made in favor of the ministers of the Lord at the expense of families and relations.

WORLD

To the mind of a devout Christian the world is the most hateful thing in the world. He withdraws himself from it, and shuns it, and concentrates all his hopes and aspirations on the world to come, and endows with all his worldly goods the priests, whose kingdom is not of this world.

YOKE

The yoke of the Lord is easy and his burden is light. To bear it we need only a strong backbone, a robust pair of shoulders, and the renunciation of all our worldly goods in favor of those who put it on us.

ZEAL

A holy fever accompanied with violent paroxysms and light-headedness, to which the pious of both sexes are subject. It is an endemial and contagious disease bestowed by Christianism on the human race. For eighteen hundred years the Christians have had good cause to rejoice in the wholesome afflictions brought down by the Son of God and his priests on the human race, and which, if God the father and the princes of the earth do not put a stop to, will infallibly go on afflicting them to the end of all time.

Subscribe to FATE Magazine Today!

- Ancient Mysteries
- Alien Abductions
- UFOs
- Atlantis
- Alternative Archaeology
- Lost Civilizations
- And more ...

FATE covers it all like no else. Published since 1948, FATE is the longest-running publication of its kind in the world, supplying its loyal readers with a broad array of true accounts of the strange and unknown for more than 63 years. FATE is a full-color, 120-page, bimonthly magazine that brings you exciting, in-depth coverage of the world's mysterious and unexplained phenomena.

1-year subscription only $27.95
Call 1-800-728-2730 or visit *www.fatemag.com*

Green Subscriptions. E-issues.
Only $39.95 for the entire year!
Go green. Save a tree, and save money.

12 issues of FATE delivered electronically to your computer for less than $3.95 an issue. • Receive twice as many issues as a print subscription. Includes six regular issues plus six theme issues (UFOs; Ghosts; Cryptozoology & Monsters; Nature Spirits & Spirituality; Strange Places & Sacred Sites; and Life After Death). • Free membership in FATE E-club (save $10). • Free all-access to Hilly Rose shows (save $12.95). • Members-only video interviews. • Discounts on all FATE merchandise. • Monthly Special Offers.

www.ingramcontent.com/pod-product-compliance
Lightning Source LLC
Chambersburg PA
CBHW070606050426
42450CB00011B/3008